FORTRESS
OF THE
MUSLIM

Du'ā from the Qur'ān & Sunnah

Sa'īd bin Ali bin Wahaf
Al-Qahtāni

Darussalam International

Published by
Darussalam International
Publications Ltd
London E10 7JN
United Kingdom

————◆————

t: +44 (0)20 8539 4885
e: info@darussalam.com
www.darussalam.com

————◆————

Contents

Transliteration

In transliterating Arabic words the following system of symbols has been used:

Arabic Script	English Symbol	Words with similar sounds
أ	' ***	-
ب	b	bless
ت	t	true
ج	j	judge
ح	h**	-
خ	kh	-
د	d	dear
ذ	<u>th</u>	this
ر	r	road
ز	z	zoo
س	s	safe
ش	sh	show
ص	s**	-
ض	dh**	-
ط	t **	-
ظ	<u>dh</u>**	-
ع	' ***	-
غ	gh	-

Arabic Script	English Symbol	Words with similar sounds
ف	f	free
ق	q **	-
ك	k	kick
ل	l	light
م	m	moon
ن	n	nice
ه	h	health
و	w	wealth
ي	y	youth

*   This symbol represents a glottal stop (transliterated medially and finally and not represented in transliteration when initial).

**   These sounds have no equivalent sounds in English.

***   The Arabic sounds represented by the symbols ('/') and the ones mentioned in the previous note are to be learned by imitating the native speakers of Arabic, if one wants to be exact in their pronunciation.

Introduction

Surely all praise is for Allāh. We praise Him and seek His help. We seek His forgiveness and we seek refuge in Him from the evil of our own souls and from the wickedness of our deeds. Whomever He guides shall never go astray, and whomever He allows to stray shall never find guidance. I bear witness that none has the right to be worshipped but Allāh, alone, Who has no partner, and I bear witness that Muhammad ﷺ is His slave and His Messenger. May the peace and blessings of Allāh be upon him and upon his family and his Companions and upon those who follow them in piety until the Day of Judgement.

This book[1] is an abridgment of my earlier work entitled, _Ath-Thikr wad-Du'a wal-‘_

---

1. _Hisnul-Muslim min ’Athkaril-Kitab was-Sunnah,_ seventeenth edition printed in the month of _Thul-Qa‘dah,_ 1416 H.

Ilāj bir-Ruqā minal-Kitāb was-Sunnah.
In order to make it small and easily portable,
I have chosen only the section on words of
remembrance for this abridgment. To achieve
this, I only mentioned the text of the words of
remembrance instead of the entire *Hadith*.

I also limited myself to mentioning only one
or two references from the original book for
each *Hadith*. Whoever would like to know
about the Companion who related a particular
Hadith, or more information about where it
is recorded, should refer to the original work
(mentioned above).

I ask Allāh the Glorious, the Mighty, by His
beautiful Names and by His sublime Attributes
to accept this as having been done sincerely
for His sake alone. I ask Him to bring me
its benefits during my lifetime and after my
death. May those who read it, those who
print it, or have had any role in distributing it,
benefit from it also. Surely He, the Glorified,
is Capable of all things.

May the peace and blessings of Allāh be upon our Prophet Muhammad, and upon his family and Companions and whoever follows them in piety until the Day of Judgement.

Saʿīd bin Ali bin Wahaf Al-Qahtāni

Safar, 1409 H

The Virtue of Remembering Allāh

Allāh the All-Mighty says:

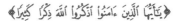

"Therefore remember Me. I will remember you.
Be grateful to Me and never show Me
ingratitude."[1]

And He says:

﴿يَـٰٓأَيُّهَا ٱلَّذِينَ ءَامَنُوا۟ ٱذْكُرُوا۟ ٱللَّهَ ذِكْرًا كَثِيرًا﴾

"O you who believe, remember Allāh with
much remembrance."[2]

And He says:

---

1. *Al-Baqarah* 2:152. Meanings of *'Ayāt* from the
   Qur'ān in this book are based on *The Interpretation of
   the Meanings of the Noble Qur'ān*, by Dr. Muhammad
   Muhsin Khan, Darussalam, Riyadh, 1994.

2. Al-Ahzāb 33:41.

﴿وَالذَّاكِرِينَ اللَّهَ كَثِيرًا وَالذَّاكِرَاتِ أَعَدَّ اللَّهُ لَهُم مَّغْفِرَةً وَأَجْرًا عَظِيمًا﴾

"And the men and women who remember Allāh frequently, Allāh has prepared for them forgiveness and a great reward."[3]

And He says:

﴿وَاذْكُر رَّبَّكَ فِي نَفْسِكَ تَضَرُّعًا وَخِيفَةً وَدُونَ الْجَهْرِ مِنَ الْقَوْلِ بِالْغُدُوِّ وَالْآصَالِ وَلَا تَكُن مِّنَ الْغَافِلِينَ﴾

"And remember your Lord by your tongue and within yourself, humbly and in awe, without loudness, by words in the morning and in the afternoon, and be not among those who are neglectful.[4]

---

3. Al-Aḥzāb 33:35.
4. Al-A'rāf 7:205.

The Prophet ﷺ said: "He who remembers his Lord and he who does not remember his Lord, are like the living and the dead."[5]

And he said, "Shall I not inform you all of the best of your works, the purest of them with your Master (Allāh), the loftiest of them in your stations, the thing that is better for you than spending gold and silver (in charity), and better for you than meeting your enemies and slaying them and being slain by them?" They (the Companions) said, "Of course!" He said, "Remembrance of Allāh, the Most High."[6]

And he said : "Allāh the Most High says, 'I am with my slave when he thinks of Me and I am with him when he mentions Me. For if he mentions Me to himself, I mention him to Myself; and if he mentions Me in a gathering,

---

5. Al-Bukhāri, cf., Al-Asqalāni, *Fathul-Bāri* 11/208; Muslim 1/539 with the wording: "The house in which Allāh is remembered and the house in which Allāh is not remembered are like the living and the dead."

6. At-Tirmithi 5/459, Ibn Mājah 2/1245. See Al-Albāni, *Sahīh Ibn Mājah* 2/316 and *Sahīh At-Tirmithi* 3/139.

I mention him in a superior gathering. If he approaches Me by a hand's width, I approach him by an arm's length; and if he approaches me by an arm's length, I approach him by two arms' length. And if he comes to Me walking, I hasten to him swiftly.'"[7]

Abdullah bin Busr ﷺ said that a man asked the Prophet ﷺ, "O Messenger of Allāh! Verily, the sanctions of Islam have become too numerous for me (to perform them all). Inform me of something (simple) that I may always adhere to." The Prophet ﷺ said, "Let your tongue always be moist with the remembrance of Allāh."[8]

And he ﷺ said : "Whoever reads one letter from the Book of Allāh, will receive one *Hasanah* (reward for a good deed), and one *Hasanah* comes with ten like it. I do not say

---

7. Al-Bukhāri 8/171, Muslim 4/2061; this wording is from Al-Bukhāri.
8. At-Tirmithi 5/175. See Al-Albāni, *Sahīh At-Tirmithi* 3/9 and *Sahīhul-Jāmi' As-Saghīr* 5/340.

that *Alif Lam-Mim* is a letter. Indeed *Alif* is a letter, and *Lam* is a letter, and *Mim* is a letter.

'Uqbah bin 'Amir ﷺ said: The Messenger of Allāh ﷺ came out (from his house) and we were on the porch *(As-Suffah).* So he said, "Who of you would like to go out in the morning every-day to the valley of *Buthan* or *Al-'Aqeeq* and come back with two large she camels without committing any sin or severing the family ties?" We replied, "O Messenger of Allāh! All of us would like this." So he said, "Would one of you not go to the *Masjid* and learn or recite two Verses from the Book of Allāh, the Mighty and Majestic? That would be better for him than two she camels. And three Verses would be better for him than three she-camels. And four Verses would be better than four she-camels, and whatever their number may be of camels."[9]

And he ﷺ said: ''Whoever sits and does not mention the Name of Allāh (before he rises),

---

9. Muslim 1/553.

will find it a cause of sorrow from Allāh. Whoever lies down to sleep and does not mention the Name of Allāh before rising, will find it a cause of sorrow from Allāh."[10]

And the Prophet ﷺ said: "No people sit in an assembly without mentioning Allāh, and without asking Allāh for blessings on their Prophet, except that it will be a cause of sorrow upon them. Thus, if He (Allāh) wishes He will punish them, and if He wishes He will forgive them."[11]

And he said: "No people may rise from an assembly in which they have failed to mention the Name of Allāh without it being as if they were getting off a dead donkey's rotting back, and it would be a cause of grief for them."[12]

---

10. Abu Dawud 4/264. See Al-Albāni, *Sahīhul-Jāmi' As-Saghīr* 5/342.

11. At-Tirmithi. See Al-Albāni, *Sahīh At-Tirmithi* 3/140.

12. Abu Dawud 4/264, Ahmad 2/389. See Al Albāni, *Sahīhul-Jami'* 5/176.

1. When you wake up

١ –«الْحَمْدُ للهِ الَّذِي أَحْيَانَا بَعْدَ مَا أَمَاتَنَا وَإِلَيْهِ النُّشُورُ»

Alhamdu lillaahil-lathee 'ahyaanaa ba'da maa 'amaatanaa wa'ilayhin-nushoor.

Praise is to Allāh Who gives us life after He has caused us to die and to Him is the return.[13]

• • •

٢ –«لَا إِلَهَ إِلَّا اللهُ وَحْدَهُ لَا شَرِيكَ لَهُ، لَهُ الْمُلْكُ وَلَهُ الْحَمْدُ، وَهُوَ عَلَى كُلِّ شَيْءٍ قَدِيرٌ. سُبْحَانَ اللهِ، وَالْحَمْدُ للهِ، وَلَا إِلَهَ إِلَّا اللهُ، وَاللهُ أَكْبَرُ، وَلَا حَوْلَ وَلَا قُوَّةَ إِلَّا بِاللهِ الْعَلِيِّ الْعَظِيمِ، رَبِّ اغْفِرْلِي».

Laa 'ilaaha 'illallaahu wahdahu laa-shareeka lahu, lahul-mulku wa lahul-hamdu, wa Huwa 'alaa kulli shay'in Qadeer. Subhaanallaahi, wal-hamdu lillaahi, wa laa 'ilaaha 'illallaahu, wal-laahu 'akbar, wa laa hawla wa laa Quwwata 'illaa billaahil 'Aliyyil-'Adheem, Rabbighfir lee.

---

13. Al-Bukhāri, cf. Al-Asqalāni, *Fathul-Bāri* 11/113; Muslim 4/2083.

There is none worthy of worship but Allāh alone, Who has no partner. His is the dominion and to Him belongs all praise, and He is Able to do all things. Glory is to Allāh. Praise is to Allāh. There is none worthy of worship but Allāh. Allāh is the Most Great. There is no might and no power except by Allāh's leave, the Exalted, the Mighty. My Lord, forgive me.[14]

٣-«الْحَمْدُ لِلهِ الَّذِي عَافَاني فِي جَسَدِي، وَرَدَّ عَلَيَّ رُوحِي، وَأَذِنَ لِي بِذِكْرِهِ»

Alhamdu lillaahil-lathee 'aafaanee fee jasadee, wa radda 'alayya roohee, wa 'athina lee bithikrihi.

Praise is to Allāh Who gave strength to my body and returned my soul to me and permitted me to remember Him.[15]

---

14. Whoever says this will be forgiven, and if he supplicates Allāh, his prayer will be answered; if he performs ablution and prays, his prayer will be accepted. Al-Bukhāri, cf. Al-Asqalāni, *Fathul Bāri* 3/39, among others. The wording here is from Ibn Mājah 2/335.

15. At-Tirmithi 5/473. See Al-Albāni's *Sahīh At-Tirmithi* 3/144.

٤ - ﴿إِنَّ فِي خَلْقِ ٱلسَّمَٰوَٰتِ وَٱلْأَرْضِ وَٱخْتِلَٰفِ ٱلَّيْلِ وَٱلنَّهَارِ لَءَايَٰتٍ لِّأُوْلِي ٱلْأَلْبَٰبِ ۞ ٱلَّذِينَ يَذْكُرُونَ ٱللَّهَ قِيَٰمًا وَقُعُودًا وَعَلَىٰ جُنُوبِهِمْ وَيَتَفَكَّرُونَ فِي خَلْقِ ٱلسَّمَٰوَٰتِ وَٱلْأَرْضِ رَبَّنَا مَا خَلَقْتَ هَٰذَا بَٰطِلًا سُبْحَٰنَكَ فَقِنَا عَذَابَ ٱلنَّارِ ۞ رَبَّنَا إِنَّكَ مَن تُدْخِلِ ٱلنَّارَ فَقَدْ أَخْزَيْتَهُۥ وَمَا لِلظَّٰلِمِينَ مِنْ أَنصَارٍ ۞ رَبَّنَا إِنَّنَا سَمِعْنَا مُنَادِيًا يُنَادِي لِلْإِيمَٰنِ أَنْ ءَامِنُواْ بِرَبِّكُمْ فَءَامَنَّا رَبَّنَا فَٱغْفِرْ لَنَا ذُنُوبَنَا وَكَفِّرْ عَنَّا سَيِّئَاتِنَا وَتَوَفَّنَا مَعَ ٱلْأَبْرَارِ ۞ رَبَّنَا وَءَاتِنَا مَا وَعَدتَّنَا عَلَىٰ رُسُلِكَ وَلَا تُخْزِنَا يَوْمَ ٱلْقِيَٰمَةِ إِنَّكَ لَا تُخْلِفُ ٱلْمِيعَادَ ۞ فَٱسْتَجَابَ لَهُمْ رَبُّهُمْ أَنِّي لَا أُضِيعُ عَمَلَ عَٰمِلٍ مِّنكُم مِّن ذَكَرٍ أَوْ أُنثَىٰ بَعْضُكُم مِّنۢ بَعْضٍ فَٱلَّذِينَ هَاجَرُواْ وَأُخْرِجُواْ مِن دِيَٰرِهِمْ وَأُوذُواْ فِي سَبِيلِي وَقَٰتَلُواْ وَقُتِلُواْ لَأُكَفِّرَنَّ عَنْهُمْ سَيِّئَاتِهِمْ وَلَأُدْخِلَنَّهُمْ جَنَّٰتٍ تَجْرِي مِن تَحْتِهَا ٱلْأَنْهَٰرُ ثَوَابًا مِّنْ عِندِ ٱللَّهِ وَٱللَّهُ عِندَهُۥ حُسْنُ ٱلثَّوَابِ ۞ لَا يَغُرَّنَّكَ تَقَلُّبُ ٱلَّذِينَ كَفَرُواْ فِي ٱلْبِلَٰدِ ۞ مَتَٰعٌ قَلِيلٌ ثُمَّ مَأْوَىٰهُمْ جَهَنَّمُ وَبِئْسَ ٱلْمِهَادُ ۞ لَٰكِنِ ٱلَّذِينَ ٱتَّقَوْاْ رَبَّهُمْ لَهُمْ جَنَّٰتٌ تَجْرِي مِن تَحْتِهَا ٱلْأَنْهَٰرُ خَٰلِدِينَ فِيهَا نُزُلًا مِّنْ عِندِ ٱللَّهِ وَمَا عِندَ ٱللَّهِ خَيْرٌ لِّلْأَبْرَارِ ۞ وَإِنَّ مِنْ أَهْلِ ٱلْكِتَٰبِ لَمَن يُؤْمِنُ بِٱللَّهِ وَمَا أُنزِلَ إِلَيْكُمْ وَمَا أُنزِلَ إِلَيْهِمْ خَٰشِعِينَ لِلَّهِ لَا يَشْتَرُونَ بِءَايَٰتِ ٱللَّهِ ثَمَنًا قَلِيلًا أُوْلَٰئِكَ

لَهُمۡ أَجۡرُهُمۡ عِندَ رَبِّهِمۡ إِنَّ ٱللَّهَ سَرِيعُ ٱلۡحِسَابِ ٥
يَٰٓأَيُّهَا ٱلَّذِينَ ءَامَنُواْ ٱصۡبِرُواْ وَصَابِرُواْ وَرَابِطُواْ وَٱتَّقُواْ ٱللَّهَ
لَعَلَّكُمۡ تُفۡلِحُونَ ﴾

'Inna fee khalqis-samaawaati wal'ardhi
wakhtilaafil-layli wannahaari la'aayaatil-li
'oolil-'albaab. Allatheena yathkuroon-allaaha
qiyaaman wa qu'oodan wa 'alaa junoobihim
wa yatafakkaroona fee khalqis-samaawaati
wal'ardhi Rabbanaa maa khalaqta haathaa
baatilan subhaanaka faqinaa 'athaaban naar.
Rabbanaa 'innaka man tudkhilin-naara faqad
'akhzaytahu wa maa lidhdhalimeena min
'ansaar. Rabbanaa 'innanaa sami'naa mu-
naadiyan yunaadee lil'eemaani 'an 'aaminoo
birabbikum fa'aamannaa, Rabbanaa faghfir
lanaa thunoobanaa wa kaffir 'annaa sayyi'aatinaa wa tawaffanaa ma'al-'abraar. Rabbanaa
wa 'aatinaa maa wa'adtanaa 'alaa rusulika wa
laa tukhzinaa yawmal-qiyaamati, 'innaka laa
tukhliful mee'aad. Fastajaaba lahum Rabbu-
hum 'annee laa 'udhee'u 'amala 'aamilim-min-
kum min thakarin 'aw 'unthaa, ba'dhukum
mim ba'dh, fallatheena haajaroo wa 'ukhrijoo

*min diyaarihim wa 'oothoo fee sabeelee wa
qaataloo wa qutiloo la'ukaffiranna 'anhum
sayyi'aatihim wa la'udkhilannahum jannaatin
tajree min tahtihal-'anhaaru thawaban min
'indillah, wallahu 'indahu husnuth-thawaab.
Laa yaghur-rannaka taqallubul-latheena
kafaroo fil-bilaad. Mataa'un qaleelun thumma ma'waahum jahannam, wa bi'sal-mihaad.
Laakinil latheenat-taqaw Rabbahum lahum
jannaatun tajree min tahtihal-'anhaaru khaal-
ideena feehaa nuzulam-min 'indillaah, wa maa
'indallaahi khayrul-lil'abraar. Wa 'inna min
'ahlil-kitaabi laman yu'minu billaahi wa maa
'unzila 'ilaykum wa maa 'unzila 'ilayhim khaash-
hi'eena lillaahi laa yashtaroona bi'aayaatillaahi
thamanan qaleela, 'oolaa'ika lahum 'ajruhum
'inda Rabbihim, 'innallaaha saree'ul-hisaab.
Yaa'ayyuhal-latheena 'aamanus-biroo wa
saabiroo wa raabitoo wattaqul-laaha la'alla-
kum tuflihoon.*

Verily! In the creation of the heavens and the
earth, and in the alternation of night and day,
there are indeed Signs for men of understand-

ing. Those who remember Allāh standing, sitting and lying down on their sides, and think deeply about the creation of the heavens and the earth, (saying:) "Our Lord! You have not created this without purpose, glory is to You! Give us salvation from the torment of the Fire. Our Lord! Verily, whom You admit to the Fire, indeed, You have disgraced him, and never will the oppressors find any helpers. Our Lord! Verily, we have heard the call of one calling to Faith (saying:) 'Believe in your Lord,' and we have believed. Our Lord! Forgive us our sins and expiate from us our evil deeds, and make us die in the state of righteousness together with the pious and righteous slaves. Our Lord! Grant us what You promised us through Your Messengers, and disgrace us not on the Day of Resurrection, for You never break (Your) promise." So, their Lord answered them (saying): "Never will I allow to be lost the work of any of you, be he male or female. You issue forth one from another, so those who emigrated and were driven out from their homes, and suffered harm in My Cause and who fought, and were killed in My Cause, verily, I will expiate from them their evil deeds and admit them into Gardens under which rivers flow; a reward from Allāh, and with Allāh is the best of rewards." Let not the free disposal of the disbelievers throughout the land deceive you. A brief enjoyment; then, their ultimate abode is Hell; and worst indeed is that place for rest. But, for those who fear their Lord, are Gardens under which rivers flow; therein are they to dwell forever, and entertainment from Allāh; and that which is with Allāh is the best for the pious and righteous slaves. And there are, certainly, among the people of the Scripture, those who believe in Allāh and in that which has been revealed to you, and in that which has been revealed to them, humbling themselves before Allāh. They do not sell the Verses of Allāh for a little price, for them is a reward with their Lord. Surely, Allāh is Swift in account. O you who believe! Have patience and contend in patience, be vigilant and informed, and fear Allāh, so that you may be successful.[16]

---

16. Qur'ān Aal-'Imrān 3:190-200; Al-Bukhāri, cf. Al-Asqalani, Fathul-Bāri 8/237; Muslim 1/530.

2. When getting dressed

٥-«الْحَمْدُ للهِ الَّذِي كَسَانِي هَذَا (الثَّوبَ) وَرَزَقَنِيهِ مِن غَيرِ
حَوْلٍ مِنِّي وَلَا قُوَّةٍ. .».

*Alhamdu lillaahil-lathee kasaanee haathaa
(aththawba) wa razaqaneehi min ghayri hawl-
im-minnee wa laa quwwatin.*

Praise is to Allāh Who has clothed me with
this (garment) and provided it for me, though
I was powerless myself and incapable.[17]

------•------

3. When putting on new clothes

٦-«اللَّهُمَّ لَكَ الْحَمْدُ أَنْتَ كَسَوْتَنِيهِ، أَسْأَلُكَ مِنْ خَيْرِهِ
وَخَيْرِ مَا صُنِعَ لَهُ، وَأَعُوذُ بِكَ مِنْ شَرِّهِ وَشَرِّ مَا صُنِعَ لَهُ».

*Allaahumma lakal-hamdu 'Anta kasawtaneehi,
'as'aluka min khayrihi wa khayri maa suni'a
lahu, wa 'a'oothu bika min sharrihi wa sharri
ma suni'a lahu.*

------

17. Al-Bukhari, Muslim, Abu Dawud, Ibn Mājah, At-
Tirmithi. See also *'Irwa'ul-Ghalīl* 7/47.

O Allāh, praise is to You. You have clothed me. I ask You for its goodness and the goodness of what it has been made for, and I seek Your protection from the evil of it and the evil of what it has been made for.[18]

---

4. For someone with new clothes

٧-«تُبْلِي وَيُخْلِفُ اللهُ تَعَالَى» .

Tublee wa yukhliful-laahu ta'aalaa.

May Allāh replace it when it is worn out.[19]

٨-«الْبَسْ جَدِيدًا، وَعِشْ حَمِيدًا، وَمُتْ شَهِيدًا» .

Ilbas jadeedan, wa 'ish hameedan, wa mut shaheedan.

---

18. Abu Dawud and At-Tirmithi. See also Al-Albāni, *Mukhtasar Shamā'il At-Tirmithi* p. 47.

19. Abu Dawud 4/41. See also Al-Albāni *Sahīh Abu Dawud* 2/760.

Put on new clothes, live a praise-worthy life and die as a martyr.[20]

---◆---

5. When undressing

«بِسْمِ اللهِ» . ٩-

9. *Bismillaahi.* In the Name of Allāh.[21]

---◆---

6. When entering the toilet

١٠-[بِسْمِ اللهِ] اللَّهُمَّ إِنِّي أَعُوذُ بِكَ مِنَ الْخُبْثِ وَالْخَبَائِثِ» .

[Bismillaahi] Allaahumma 'innee' 'a'oothu bika minal-khubthi walkhabaa'ith.

(*Before entering*) [In the Name of Allāh].

---

20. Ibn Mājah 2/1178, Al-Baghawi 12/41. See also Al-Albāni, *Sahīh Ibn Mājah* 2/275.

21. At-Tirmithi 2/505, among others. *See 'Irwa'ul-Ghalil* no. 49 and *Sahīhul-Jāmi'* 3/203.

(*Then*) O Allāh, I seek protection in You from the male and female unclean spirits. [22]

--------------◆--------------

7. When leaving the toilet

١١ –«غُفْرَانَكَ» .

Ghufraanaka. I seek Your forgiveness. [23]

--------------◆--------------

8. Before performing ablution

١٢ –«بِسْمِ اللهِ» .

Bismillaahi. In the Name of Allāh.[24]

---

22. Al-Bukhāri 1/45, Muslim 1/283. The addition of *Bismillāh* at its beginning was reported by Sa‘id bin Mansūr. See *Fathul-Bāri* 1/244.

23. Abu Dawud, Ibn Mājah and At-Tirmithi. An Nasā’i recorded it in ‘*Amalul-Yawm wal-Laylah*. Also see the checking of Ibn Al-Qayyim’s *Zādul-Ma‘ād*, 2/387.

24. Abu Dawud, Ibn Mājah, and Aḥmad. See also Al-Albāni, ’*Irwa’ul-Ghalil* 1/122.

9. Upon completing ablution

١٣-«أَشْهَدُ أَنْ لَا إِلَهَ إِلَّا اللهُ وَحْدَهُ لَا شَرِيكَ لَهُ، وَأَشْهَدُ
أَنَّ مُحَمَّدًا عَبْدُهُ وَرَسُولُهُ..».

*'Ash-hadu 'an laa 'ilaaha 'illallaahu wahdahu
laa shareeka lahu wa'ash-hadu 'anna Muhammadan 'abduhu wa Rasooluhu.*

I bear witness that none has the right to be
worshipped but Allāh alone, Who has no partner; and I bear witness that Muhammad is His
slave and His Messenger.[25]

* * *

١٤-«اللَّهُمَّ اجْعَلْنِي مِنَ التَّوَّابِينَ وَاجْعَلْنِي مِنَ
الْمُتَطَهِّرِينَ».

*Allaahummaj'alnee minat-tawwaabeena
waj'alnee minal-mutatahhireen.*

O Allāh, make me among those who turn to

---

25. Muslim 1/209.

You in repentance, and make me among those who are purified.[26]

•

١٥–«سُبْحَانَكَ اللّٰهُمَّ وَبِحَمْدِكَ، أَشْهَدُ أَنْ لَا إِلَهَ إِلَّا أَنْتَ، أَسْتَغْفِرُكَ وَأَتُوبُ إِلَيْكَ».

Subhaanaka Allaahumma wa bihamdika, 'ash-hadu 'an laa 'ilaaha 'illaa 'Anta, 'astaghfiruka wa 'atoobu 'ilayk.

Glory is to You, O Allāh, and praise; I bear witness that there is none worthy of worship but You. I seek Your forgiveness and turn to You in repentance.[27]

•

---

26. At-Tirmithi 1/78. See also Al-Albāni, *Saḥīḥ* At-Tirmithi 1/18.

27. An-Nasā'i, 'Amalul-Yawmwal-Laylah, p.173. See also Al-Albāni, 'Irwa'ul-Ghalīl 1/135 and 2/94.

10. When leaving your home

١٦ –«بِسْمِ اللهِ، تَوَكَّلْتُ عَلَى اللهِ، وَلَا حَوْلَ وَلَا قُوَّةَ إِلَّا بِاللهِ».

Bismillaahi, tawakkaltu 'alallaahi, wa laa hawla walaa quwwata 'illaa billaah.

In the Name of Allāh, I have placed my trust in Allāh, there is no might and no power except by Allāh.[28]

❖

١٧ –«اللَّهُمَّ إِنِّي أَعُوذُ بِكَ أَنْ أَضِلَّ، أَوْ أُضَلَّ، أَوْ أَزِلَّ، أَوْ أُزَلَّ، أَوْ أَظْلِمَ، أَوْ أُظْلَمَ، أَوْ أَجْهَلَ، أَوْ يُجْهَلَ عَلَيَّ».

Allaahumma 'innee 'a'oothu bika 'an 'adhilla, 'aw 'udhalla, 'aw 'azilla, 'aw 'uzalla, 'aw 'adh-lima, 'aw 'udhlama, 'aw 'ajhala 'aw yujhala 'alayya.

O Allāh, I seek refuge in You lest I misguide others, or I am misguided by others, lest I

---

28. Abu Dawud 4/325, At-Tirmithi 5/490. See also Al-Al-bāni, *Sahīh At-Tirmithi* 3/151.

cause others to err or I am caused to err, lest
I abuse others or be abused, and lest I behave
foolishly or meet with the foolishness of others.[29]

-------------◆-------------

11. When entering your home

١٨ -«بِسْمِ اللهِ وَلَجْنَا، وَبِسْمِ اللهِ خَرَجْنَا، وَعَلَى رَبِّنَا تَوَكَّلْنَا».

*Bismillaahi walajnaa, wa bismillaahi kharajnaa,
wa 'alaa Rabbinaa tawakkalnaa.*

In the Name of Allāh we enter, in the Name of
Allāh we leave, and on our Lord we depend [then
say *As-Salaamu 'Alaykum* to those present]. [30]

-------------◆-------------

29. Abu Dawud, Ibn Mājah, An-Nasā'i, At-Tirmithi.
    See also Al-Albāni, *Saḥīḥ At-Tirmithi* 3/152 and *Saḥīḥ
    Ibn Mājah* 2/336.
30. Abu Dawud 4/325. Muslim (Hadith no. 2018) says that
    one should mention the Name of Allāh when entering
    the home and when beginning to eat; and that the
    devil, hearing this, says: "There is no shelter for us here
    tonight and no food."

12. When going to the *Masjid*

١٩ –"اللَّهُمَّ اجْعَل فِي قَلْبِي نُورًا، وَفِي لِسَانِي نُورًا، وَفِي
سَمْعِي نُورًا، وَفِي بَصَرِي نُورًا، وَمِنْ فَوْقِي نُورًا، وَمِنْ
تَحْتِي نُورًا، وَعَنْ يَمِينِي نُورًا، وَعَنْ شِمَالِي نُورًا، وَمِنْ
أَمَامِي نُورًا، وَمِنْ خَلْفِي نُورًا، وَاجْعَل فِي نَفْسِي نُورًا،
وَأَعْظِمْ لِي نُورًا، وَعَظِّمْ لِي نُورًا، وَاجْعَل لِي نُورًا،
وَاجْعَلْنِي نُورًا، وَاجْعَل فِي عَصَبِي
نُورًا، وَفِي لَحْمِي نُورًا، وَفِي دَمِي نُورًا، وَفِي شَعْرِي
نُورًا، وَفِي بَشَرِي نُورًا." "[اللَّهُمَّ اجْعَل لِي نُورًا فِي
قَبْرِي.. وَنُورًا فِي عِظَامِي]" [وَزِدْنِي نُورًا، وَزِدْنِي
نُورًا، وَزِدْنِي نُورًا"] [وَهَبْ لِي نُورًا عَلَى نُورٍ"].

*Allaahummaj'al fee qalbee nooran, wa fee
lisaanee nooran, wa fee sam'ee nooran, wa fee
basaree nooran, wa min fawqee nooran, wa
min tahtee nooran, wa 'an yameenee nooran,
wa 'an shimaalee nooran, wa min 'amaamee
nooran, wa min khalfee nooran, waj'alfee nafsee nooran, wa 'a<u>dh</u>im lee nooran, wa 'a<u>dh</u>-
<u>dh</u>im lee nooran, waj'al lee nooran, waj'al nee
nooran, Allaahumma 'a'tinee nooran, waj'al
fee 'asabee nooran, wa fee lahmee nooran,
wa fee damee nooran, wa fee sha'ree nooran,*

wa fee basharee nooran. [Allaahummaj'al lee nooran fee qabree wa nooranfee 'idhaamee.] [Wa zidnee nooran, wa zidnee nooran, wa zidnee nooran.] [Wa hab lee nooran 'alaa noor.]

O Allāh, place light in my heart, and on my tongue light, and in my ears light and in my sight light, and above me light, and below me light, and to my right light, and to my left light, and before me light and behind me light. Place in my soul light. Magnify for me light, and amplify for me light. Make for me light and make me a light. O Allāh, grant me light, and place light in my nerves, and in my body light and in my blood light and in my hair light and in my skin light.[31] [O Allāh, make for me a light in my grave... and a light in my bones.][32] [Increase me in light, increase me in light, increase me in light.][33] [Grant me light upon light.][34]

---

31. Up to this point was reported by Al-Bukhāri 11/116 (Hadith no. 6316) and by Muslim 1/526, 529-530 (Hadith no. 763).

32. At-Tirmithi 5/483 (Hadith no. 3419).

33. Al-Bukhāri in *Al-'Adab Al-Mufrad* (Hadith no. 695), p. 258. See also Al-Albāni, *Sahīh Al-'Adab Al-Mufrad* (no. 536).

34. Al-Bukhāri, cf. Al-Asqalāni, *Fathul-Bāri* 11/118.

13. When entering the *Masjid*

٢٠-«أَعُوذُ بِاللهِ الْعَظِيمِ، وَبِوَجْهِهِ الْكَرِيمِ، وَسُلْطَانِهِ
الْقَدِيمِ، مِنَ الشَّيْطَانِ الرَّجِيمِ». [بِسمِ اللهِ، وَالصَّلَاةُ]
[وَالسَّلَامُ عَلَى رَسُولِ اللهِ] «اللَّهُمَّ افْتَحْ لِي أَبْوَابَ رَحْمَتِكَ».

'A'oo*th*u billaahil-'A*dh*eem, wa bi Wajhihil-
Kareem, wa Sultaanihil-qadeem, minash-Shaytaanir-rajeem.

[Bismillaahi, wassalaatu.]
[Wassalaamu 'alaa Rasoolillaahi.]

Allaahum-maftahlee'abwaabarahmatika.

I seek refuge in Almighty Allāh, by His Noble
Face, by His primordial power, from Satan the
outcast. [35] [In the Name of Allāh, and blessings.][36] [And peace be upon the Messenger of

---

35. Abu Dawud and Al-Albāni, *Sahīhul-Jami' As Saghir*
(Hadith no. 4591).
36. Ibn As-Sunni (Hadith no. 88), graded good by Al-
Albāni.

Allāh.[37] O Allāh, open before me the doors of Your mercy.[38]

•

---

14. When leaving the *Masjid*

٢١-«بِسْمِ اللهِ وَالصَّلَاةُ وَالسَّلَامُ عَلَى رَسُولِ اللهِ، اللَّهُمَّ إِنِّي أَسْأَلُكَ مِنْ فَضْلِكَ، اللَّهُمَّ اعْصِمْنِي مِنَ الشَّيْطَانِ الرَّجِيمِ».

Bismillaahi wassalaatu wassalaaamu 'alaa Rasoolillaahi, Allaahumma 'innee 'as'aluka min fadhlika, Allaahumma'simnee minash-Shaytaan-ir-rajeem.

In the Name of Allāh, and peace and blessings be upon the Messenger of Allāh. O Allāh, I

---

37. Abu Dawud 1/126, see also Al-Albāni, *Sahīhul-Jāmi' As-Saghir* 1/528.

38. Muslim 1/494. There is also a report in *Sunan Ibn Mā-jah* on the authority of Fātimah رضي الله عنها : "O Allāh, forgive me my sins and open for me the doors of Your mercy." It was graded authentic by Al-Albāni due to supporting Ahadith. See *Sahīh Ibn Mājah* 1/128-9.

ask for Your favor, O Allāh, protect me from Satan the outcast.[39]

* * *

15. On hearing the *'Athân* (call to prayer)

Repeat what the *Mu'aththin* says, except for when he says:

«حَيَّ عَلَى الصَّلاةِ وَحَيَّ عَلَى الْفَلاحِ».

Hayya 'alas-Salaah (hasten to the prayer) and *Hayya 'alal-Falaah* (hasten to salvation). Here you should say:

«لَا حَوْلَ وَلَا قُوَّةَ إِلَّا بِاللهِ».

Laa hawla wa laa quwwata 'illaa billaah.

There is no might and no power except by Allāh.[40]

---

39. Ibid.
40. Al-Bukhāri 1/152, Muslim 1/288.

٢٣-«وَأَنَا أَشْهَدُ أَنْ لَا إِلَهَ إِلَّا اللهُ وَحْدَهُ لَا شَرِيكَ لَهُ وَأَنَّ
مُحَمَّدًا عَبْدُهُ وَرَسُولُهُ، رَضِيتُ بِاللهِ رَبًّا وَبِمُحَمَّدٍ رَسُولًا
وَبِالْإِسْلَامِ دِينًا».

Wa 'anaa 'ash-hadu 'an laa 'ilaaha 'illallaahu wahdahu laa shareeka lahu wa 'anna Muhammadan 'abduhu wa Rasooluhu, radheetu billaahi Rabban, wa bi Muhammadin Rasoolan wa bil'islaami deenan.

I bear witness that none has the right to be worshipped but Allāh alone, Who has no partner, and that Muhammad is His slave and His Messenger. I am pleased with Allāh as my Lord, with Muhammad as my Messenger and with Islam as my religion.[41] [To be recited in Arabic after the *Mu'aththin's Tashahhud* or the words of affirmation of Faith].[42]

---

41. Muslim 1/290.
42. Ibn Khuzaymah 1/220.

After replying to the call of *Mu'aththin*, recite in Arabic Allāh's blessings on the Prophet.[43]

٢٥- «اللَّهُمَّ رَبَّ هَذِهِ الدَّعْوَةِ التَّامَّةِ، وَالصَّلَاةِ الْقَائِمَةِ، آتِ مُحَمَّدًا الْوَسِيلَةَ وَالْفَضِيلَةَ، وَابْعَثْهُ مَقَامًا مَحْمُودًا الَّذِي وَعَدْتَهُ.»

Allaahumma Rabba haathihid-da'watit taammati wassalaatil-qaa'imati, 'aati Muham-madanil-waseelata walfadheelata, wab'ath-hu maqaamam-mahmoodanil-lathee wa'adtahu.

O Allāh, Lord of this perfect call and established prayer. Grant Muhammad the intercession and favor, and raise him to the honored station You have promised him.

Between the call to prayer and the *'Iqamah,* you should supplicate Allāh for yourself. Invocation during this time is not rejected.[44]

---

43. Muslim 1/288.
44. At-Tirmithi, Abu Dawud, Aḥmad. See also Al-Albāni, 'Irwa'ul-Ghalīl 1/262.

16. Du'ā at the beginning of the *Salat*

٢٧-«اللَّهُمَّ بَاعِدْ بَيْنِي وَبَيْنَ خَطَايَايَ كَمَا بَاعَدْتَ بَيْنَ
الْمَشْرِقِ وَالْمَغْرِبِ، اللَّهُمَّ نَقِّنِي مِنْ خَطَايَايَ، كَمَا يُنَقَّى
الثَّوْبُ الْأَبْيَضُ مِنَ الدَّنَسِ، اللَّهُمَّ اغْسِلْنِي مِنْ خَطَايَايَ
بِالثَّلْجِ وَالْمَاءِ وَالْبَرَدِ».

*Allaahumma baa'id baynee wa bayna khataa-
yaaya kamaa baa adta baynal mashriq wal magh-
ribi, Allaahumma naqqinee min khataayaaya
kamaa yunaqqath thawbul-'abyadhu minad-
danasi, Allaahummaghsilnee min khataayaaya,
bith-thalji walmaa'i walbarad.*

O Allāh, separate me from my sins as You have
separated the East from the West. O Allāh,
cleanse me of my transgressions as the white
garment is cleansed of stains. O Allāh, wash
away my sins with ice and water and frost.[45]

---

45. Al-Bukhāri 1/181, Muslim 1/419.

٢٨-«سُبْحَانَكَ اللَّهُمَّ وَبِحَمْدِكَ، وَتَبَارَكَ اسْمُكَ، وَتَعَالَى
جَدُّكَ، وَلَا إِلَهَ غَيْرُكَ».

Subhaanaka Allaahumma wa bihamdika,
wa tabaarakasmuka, wa ta'aalaa jadduka,
wa laa 'ilaaha ghayruka.

Glory is to You O Allāh, and praise. Blessed
is Your Name and Exalted is Your Majesty.
There is none worthy of worship but You.[46]

---

46. Abu Dawud, Ibn Mājah, An-Nasā'i, At-Tirmithi. See
    Al-Albāni, *Sahīh At-Tirmithi* 1/77 and *Sahīh Ibn Mājah*
    1/135.

٢٩-«وَجَّهْتُ وَجْهِيَ لِلَّذِي فَطَرَ السَّمَوَاتِ وَالْأَرْضَ حَنِيفًا
وَمَا أَنَا مِنَ الْمُشْرِكِينَ، إِنَّ صَلَاتِي، وَنُسُكِي، وَمَحْيَايَ،
وَمَمَاتِي لِلَّهِ رَبِّ الْعَالَمِينَ، لَا شَرِيكَ لَهُ وَبِذَلِكَ أُمِرْتُ
وَأَنَا مِنَ الْمُسْلِمِينَ. اللَّهُمَّ أَنْتَ الْمَلِكُ لَا إِلَهَ إِلَّا أَنْتَ.
أَنْتَ رَبِّي وَأَنَا عَبْدُكَ، ظَلَمْتُ نَفْسِي وَاعْتَرَفْتُ بِذَنْبِي
فَاغْفِرْ لِي ذُنُوبِي جَمِيعًا إِنَّهُ لَا يَغْفِرُ الذُّنُوبَ إِلَّا أَنْتَ.
وَاهْدِنِي لِأَحْسَنِ الْأَخْلَاقِ لَا يَهْدِي لِأَحْسَنِهَا إِلَّا أَنْتَ،
وَاصْرِفْ عَنِّي سَيِّئَهَا لَا يَصْرِفُ عَنِّي سَيِّئَهَا إِلَّا أَنْتَ، لَبَّيْكَ
وَسَعْدَيْكَ، وَالْخَيْرُ كُلُّهُ بِيَدَيْكَ، وَالشَّرُّ لَيْسَ إِلَيْكَ، أَنَا
بِكَ وَإِلَيْكَ، تَبَارَكْتَ وَتَعَالَيْتَ، أَسْتَغْفِرُكَ وَأَتُوبُ إِلَيْكَ».

Wajjahtu wajhiya lilla*thee* fataras samaawaati
wal'ardha haneefan wa maa 'anaa minal- mushri-
keen, 'inna salaatee, wa nusukee, wa mahyaaya,
wa mamaatee lillaahi Rabbil- 'aalameen, laa
shareeka lahu wa bi*thaa*lika 'umirtu wa 'anaa
minal muslimeen. Allaahumma 'Antal-Maliku
laa 'ilaaha 'illaa 'Anta. 'Anta Rabbee wa 'anaa
'abduka, *dh*alamtu nafsee wa'taraftu bi*th*anbee
faghfir lee *th*unoobee jamee'an 'innahu laa
yaghfiru*th-th*unooba 'illaa 'Anta. Wahdinee

• **33** •

*li'ahsanil-'akhlaaqi laa yahdee li'ahsanihaa
'illaa 'Anta, wasrif 'annee sayyi'ahaa, laa
yasrifu 'annee sayyi'ahaa 'illa 'Anta, labbayka
wa sa'dayka, walkhayru kulluhu biyadayka,
washsharru laysa 'ilayka, 'anaa bika wa 'ilayka, tabaarakta wa ta'aalayta, 'astaghfiruka wa
'atoobu 'ilayka.*

I turn my face towards the One Who created
the heavens and the earth, as a true believer. I
am not of those who associate partners with
Allāh. Verily, my prayer and my devotion, my
living and my death, are for Allāh, Lord of the
worlds, He has no partners. Thus I have been
commanded and I am among those who have
submitted. O Allāh, You are the King, there is
none worthy of worship but You. You are my
Lord and I am Your slave. I have wronged my
own soul and confess my sin. Forgive all of my
sins, surely none forgives sins but You. Guide
me to the perfection of my character, for none
guides to its perfection but You. Protect me
from the evils of my character, for none may
protect me from its evils but You. I am here

at Your service. All goodness is in Your Hands, and evil is not attributed to You. I am (created) by You, and I am (returning) to You. You are Most Blessed, Most Exalted. I seek Your forgiveness and repent to You.[47]

------------- ♦ -------------

٣٠-«اللَّهُمَّ رَبَّ جِبْرائِيلَ، وَمِيكَائِيلَ، وَإِسْرَافِيلَ فَاطِرَ السَّمَوَاتِ وَالْأَرْضِ، عَالِمَ الْغَيْبِ وَالشَّهَادَةِ، أَنْتَ تَحْكُمُ بَيْنَ عِبَادِكَ فِيمَا كَانُوا فِيهِ يَخْتَلِفُونَ. اهْدِنِي لِمَا اخْتُلِفَ فِيهِ مِنَ الْحَقِّ بِإِذْنِكَ إِنَّكَ تَهْدِي مَنْ تَشَاءُ إِلَى صِرَاطٍ مُسْتَقِيمٍ».

Allaahumma Rabba Jibraa'eela, wa Mikaa'eela, wa 'Israafeela faatiras samaawaati wal'ardh, 'Aalimal-ghaybi washshahaadati, 'Anta tahkumu bayna 'ibaadika feemaa kaanoo feehi yakhtalifoon. Ihdinee limakh-tulifa feehi minal-haqqi bi 'ithnika 'innaka tahdee man tashaa'u 'ilaa siraatim-mustaqeem.

---

47. Muslim 1/534.

O Allāh, Lord of Jibrā'il, Mika'il and Isrāfil. Maker of the heavens and the earth. Knower of the unseen and the seen. You judge between Your slaves regarding that in which they differ. Guide me to the truth regarding that in which there is difference, by Your leave. Surely, You guide whomever you please to the straight path.[48]

---------------- ◆ ----------------

٣١-«اللهُ أَكْبَرُ كَبِيرًا، اللهُ أَكْبَرُ كَبِيرًا، اللهُ أَكْبَرُ كَبِيرًا، وَالْحَمْدُ للهِ كَثِيرًا، وَالْحَمْدُ للهِ كَثِيرًا، وَالْحَمْدُ للهِ كَثِيرًا، وَسُبْحَانَ اللهِ بُكْرَةً وَأَصِيلًا» ثَلَاثًا «أَعُوذُ بِاللهِ مِنَ الشَّيْطَانِ: مِنْ نَفْخِهِ، وَنَفْثِهِ، وَهَمْزِهِ».

Allaahu 'Akbar Kabeera, Allaahu 'Akbar Kabeera, Allaahu 'Akbar Kabeera, walhamdu lillaahi katheera, walhamdu lillaahi katheera, walhamdu lillaahi katheera, wa Subhaanallaahi bukratan wa 'aseela. 'A'oothu billaahi minash-Shaytaan: min nafkhihi, wa nafthihi, wa hamzihi.

---

48. Muslim 1/534.

Allāh is the Greatest, Most Great. Allāh is the
Greatest, Most Great. Allāh is the Greatest,
Most Great. Praise is to Allāh, abundantly.
Praise is to Allāh, abundantly. Praise is to Allāh,
abundantly. Glory is to Allāh, at the break
of day and at its end. [Recite three times in
Arabic.] I seek refuge in Allāh from Satan. From
his breath and from his voice, and from his
whisper.[49]

* ⋯⋯⋯ • ⋯⋯⋯

٣٢-«اللَّهُمَّ لَكَ الْحَمْدُ أَنْتَ نُورُ السَّمَوَاتِ وَالأَرْضِ وَمَنْ
فِيهِنَّ، وَلَكَ الْحَمْدُ أَنْتَ قَيِّمُ السَّمَوَاتِ وَالأَرْضِ وَمَنْ
فِيهِنَّ، [وَلَكَ الْحَمْدُ أَنْتَ رَبُّ السَّمَوَاتِ وَالأَرْضِ وَمَنْ
فِيهِنَّ] [وَلَكَ الْحَمْدُ لَكَ مُلْكُ السَّمَوَاتِ وَالأَرْضِ وَمَنْ
فِيهِنَّ] [وَلَكَ الْحَمْدُ أَنْتَ مَلِكُ السَّمَوَاتِ وَالأَرْضِ]
[وَلَكَ الْحَمْدُ] [أَنْتَ الْحَقُّ، وَوَعْدُكَ الْحَقُّ، وَقَوْلُكَ
الْحَقُّ، وَلِقَاؤُكَ الْحَقُّ، وَالْجَنَّةُ حَقٌّ، وَالنَّارُ حَقٌّ،
وَالنَّبِيُّونَ حَقٌّ، وَمُحَمَّدٌ ﷺ حَقٌّ، وَالسَّاعَةُ حَقٌّ] [اللَّهُمَّ

---

49. Abu Dawud 1/203, Ibn Mājah 1/265, and Aḥmad
    4/85. Muslim recorded a similar Hadith, 1/420.

لَكَ أَسْلَمْتُ ، وَعَلَيْكَ تَوَكَّلْتُ ، وَإِلَيْكَ أَنَبْتُ ، وَبِكَ خَاصَمْتُ ، وَإِلَيْكَ حَاكَمْتُ ، فَاغْفِرْ لِي مَا قَدَّمْتُ ، وَمَا أَخَّرْتُ ، وَمَا أَسْرَرْتُ ، وَمَا أَعْلَنْتُ] [أَنْتَ الْمُقَدِّمُ ، وَأَنْتَ الْمُؤَخِّرُ لَا إِلَهَ إِلَّا أَنْتَ] [أَنْتَ إِلَهِي لَا إِلَهَ إِلَّا أَنْتَ]».

*Allaahumma lakal-hamdu 'Anta noorus
samaawaati wal'ardhi wa man feehinna, wa
lakal-hamdu 'Anta qayyimus-samaawaati
wal'ardhi wa man feehinna, [wa lakal-hamdu 'Anta Rabbus-samaawaati wal'ardhi wa
man feehinna] [wa lakal-hamdu laka mulkus
samaawaati wal'ardhi wa manfeehinnaj [wa
lakal-hamdu 'Anta Malikus-samaawaati
wal'ardhi] [wa lakal-hamdu] ['Antal-haqq,
wa wa'dukal-haqq, wa qawlukal-haqq wa
liqaa'ukal-haqq, waijannatu haqq, wannaaru
haqq, wannabiyyoona haqq, wa Muham-
madun (sallallaahu 'alayhi wa sallam) haqq,
wassaa'atu haqq] [Allaahumma laka 'aslamtu,
wa 'alayka tawakkaltu, wa bika 'aamantu,
wa 'ilayka 'anabtu, wa bika khaasamtu, wa
'ilayka haakamtu. Faghfirlee maa qaddamtu,*

*wa maa 'akhkhartu, wa maa 'asrartu, wa maa
'a'lantu] ['Antal-Mu'akhkhiru, laa 'ilaaha 'illaa
'Antaj ['Anta 'ilaahee laa 'ilaaha 'illaa 'Anta].*

O Allāh, praise is to You. You are the Light
of the heavens and the earth and all that they
contain. Praise is to You, You are the Sus-
tainer of the heavens and the earth and all
they contain. [Praise is to You, You are the
Lord of the heavens and the earth and all they
contain.] [Praise is to You, Yours is dominion of the heavens and the earth and all they
contain.] [Praise is to You, You are the King
of the heavens and the earth.] [And praise is
to You.] [You are the Truth, Your Promise is
true, Your Word is true, Your audience is true,
Paradise is true, Hell is true, the Prophets are
true, and Muhammad (peace and blessings be
upon him) is true, and the Hour of Judgment is
true.] [O Allāh, to You I have submitted, and
upon You I depend. I have believed in You and
to You I turn in repentance. For Your sake I
dispute and by Your standard I judge. Forgive
me what I have sent before me and what I

have left behind me, what I have concealed and what I have declared.] [You are the One Who sends forth and You are the One Who delays, there is none who has the right to be worshipped but You.] [You are my God, there is none who has the right to be worshipped but You.][50]

---

17. When in *Ruku‘* (bowing in prayer)

٣٣-«سُبْحَانَ رَبِّيَ الْعَظِيمِ».

Subhaana Rabbiyal-‘Adheem.

Glory to my Lord the Exalted (three times in Arabic).[51]

---

50. Al-Bukhāri, cf. Al-Asqalāni, Fathul-Bāri 3/3, 11/116, 13/371, 423, 465. See also Muslim for a shorter account, 1/532.
51. Abu Dawud, Ibn Mājah, An-Nasā’i, At-Tirmithi, and Aḥmad. See Al-Albāni's *Sahīh At-Tirmithi* 1/83.

٣٤-«سُبْحَانَكَ اللَّهُمَّ رَبَّنَا وَبِحَمْدِكَ اللَّهُمَّ اغْفِرْ لِي».

Subhaanaka Allaahumma Rabbanaa wa bihamdika Allaahum-maghfir lee.

Glory is to You, O Allāh, our Lord, and praise is Yours. O Allāh, forgive me.[52]

•

٣٥-«سُبُّوحٌ، قُدُّوسٌ، رَبُّ الْمَلَائِكَةِ وَالرُّوحِ».

Subboohun, Quddoosun, Rabbul malaa'ikati warrooh.

Glory (to You), Most Holy (are You), Lord of the angels and the Spirit.[53]

•

٣٦-«اللَّهُمَّ لَكَ رَكَعْتُ، وَبِكَ آمَنْتُ، وَلَكَ أَسْلَمْتُ خَشَعَ لَكَ سَمْعِي، وَبَصَرِي وَمُخِّي، وَعَظْمِي، وَعَصَبِي، وَمَا اسْتَقَلَّ بِهِ قَدَمِي».

---

52. Al-Bukhāri 1/99, Muslim 1/350.
53. Muslim 1/353, Abu Dawud 1/230.

Allaahumma laka raka'tu, wa bika 'aamantu, wa laka 'aslamtu khasha'a laka sam'ee, wa basaree, wa mukhkhee, wa 'adhmee, wa 'asa- bee, wa mastaqalla bihi qadamee.

O Allāh, to You I bow (in prayer) and in You I believe and to You I have submitted. Before You my hearing is humbled, as is my sight, my mind, my bones, my nerves and what my feet have mounted upon (for travel).[54]

❖

٣٧-«سُبْحَانَ ذِي الْجَبَرُوتِ، وَالْمَلَكُوتِ، وَالْكِبْرِيَاءِ، وَالْعَظَمَةِ».

Subhaana thil-jabarooti, walmalakooti, wal- kibriyaa'i, wal'adhamati.

Glory is to You, Master of power, of domin- ion, of majesty and greatness.[55]

---

54. Muslim 1/534, Abu Dawud, An-Nasā'i and At- -Tirmithi.

55. Abu Dawud 1/230, An-Nasā'i and Aḥmad. Its chain of narration is good (*Hasan*).

18. When rising from *Rukú'*

٣٨-«سَمِعَ اللهُ لِمَنْ حَمِدَهُ».

Sami'allaahu liman hamidah.

Allāh hears whoever praises Him.[56]

------- ♦ -------

٣٩-رَبَّنَا وَلَكَ الْحَمْدُ، حَمْدًا كَثِيرًا طَيِّبًا مُبَارَكًا فِيهِ».

Rabbanaa wa lakal-hamd, hamdan katheeran tayyiban mubaarakan feeh.

Our Lord, praise is Yours, abundant, good and blessed praise.[57]

------- ♦ -------

56. Al-Bukhāri, cf. Al-Asqalāni, *Fathul-Bāri* 2/282.
57. A l-Bukhari, cf. Al-Asqalāni, *Fathul-Bāri* 2/284.

٤٠- «مِلْءُ السَّمٰوَاتِ وَمِلْءُ الأَرْضِ وَمَا بَيْنَهُمَا، وَمِلْءُ مَا
شِئْتَ مِنْ شَيْءٍ بَعْدُ. أَهْلَ الثَّنَاءِ وَالْمَجْدِ، أَحَقُّ مَا قَالَ
الْعَبْدُ، وَكُلُّنَا لَكَ عَبْدٌ. اللَّهُمَّ لَا مَانِعَ لِمَا أَعْطَيْتَ، وَلَا
مُعْطِيَ لِمَا مَنَعْتَ، وَلَا يَنْفَعُ ذَالْجَدِّ مِنْكَ الْجَدُّ».

*Mil'as-samaawaati wa mil'al-'ardhi wa maa
baynahumaa, wa mil'a maa shi'ta min shay'in
ba‘d. 'Ahlath-thanaa'i walmajdi, 'ahaqqu
maa qaalal-‘abdu, wa kullunaa laka ‘abdun.
Allaahumma laa maani‘a limaa 'a‘tayta, wa
laa mu‘tiya limaa mana‘ta, wa laa yanfa‘u
<u>th</u>al-jaddi minkal-jadd.*

(A praise that) fills the heavens and the earth
and what lies between them, and whatever
else You please. (You Allāh) are most worthy
of praise and majesty, and what the slave has
said – we are all Your slaves. O Allāh, there
is none who can withhold what You give, and
none may give what You have withheld. And
the might of the mighty person cannot benefit
him against You.[58]

---

58. Muslim 1/346.

19. When in *Sujood*

٤١-«سُبْحَانَ رَبِّيَ الأَعْلَى».

Subhaana Rabbiyal-A'laa

Glory is to my Lord, the Most High. (This is said three times in Arabic)[59]

◆

٤٢-«سُبْحَانَكَ اللَّهُمَّ رَبَّنَا وَبِحَمْدِكَ اللَّهُمَّ اغْفِرْ لِي».

Subhaanaka Allhumma Rabbanaa wa biham-dika Allahum-maghfir lee.

Glory is to You, O Allāh, our Lord, and praise is Yours. O Allāh, forgive me.[60]

◆

---

59. Abu Dawud, Ibn Mājah, An-Nasā'i, At-Tirmithi, and Aḥmad. see also Al-Albani, *Sahih At-Tirmithi* 1/83.

60. Al-Bukhāri and Muslim, see invocation no. 34 above.

٤٣-«سُبُّوحٌ، قُدُّوسٌ، رَبُّ الْمَلَائِكَةِ وَالرُّوحِ» .

Subboohun, Quddoosun, Rabbul malaa'ikati warrooh.

Glory (to You), Most Holy (are You), Lord of the angels and the Spirit.[61]

--------- ◆ ---------

٤٤-«اللَّهُمَّ لَكَ سَجَدْتُ وَبِكَ آمَنْتُ، وَلَكَ أَسْلَمْتُ، سَجَدَ وَجْهِيَ لِلَّذِي خَلَقَهُ، وَصَوَّرَهُ، وَشَقَّ سَمْعَهُ وَبَصَرَهُ، تَبَارَكَ اللهُ أَحْسَنُ الْخَالِقِينَ» .

Allaahumma laka sajadtu wa bika 'aamantu, wa laka 'aslamtu, sajada wajhiya lilathee khalaqahu, wa sawwarahu, wa shaqqa sam'ahu wa basarahu, tabaarakallaahu 'ahsanul-khaaliqeen.

O Allāh, to You I prostrate myself and in You I believe. To You I have submitted. My face is prostrated to the One Who created it, fash-

----

61. Muslim 1/533, see invocation no. 35 above.

ioned it, and gave it hearing and sight. Blessed is
Allāh, the Best of creators.[62]

٤٥-«سُبْحَانَ ذِي الْجَبَرُوتِ، وَالْمَلَكُوتِ، وَالْكِبْرِيَاءِ،
وَالْعَظَمَةِ».

*Subhaana thil-jabarooti, walmalakooti, wal-
kibriyaa'i, wal'adhamati.*

Glory is to You, Master of power, of dominion,
of majesty and greatness.[63]

٤٦-«اللّهُمَّ اغْفِرْ لِي ذَنْبِي كُلَّهُ، دِقَّهُ وَجِلَّهُ، وَأَوَّلَهُ وَآخِرَهُ
وَعَلَانِيَتَهُ وَسِرَّهُ»

*Allaahum-maghfir lee thanbee kullahu, diqqa-
hu wa jillahu, wa 'awwalahu wa 'aakhirahu
wa 'alaaniyatahu wa sirrahu.*

---

62. Muslim 1/534 and others.

63. Abu Dawud 1/230, An-Nasā'i, Ahmad. See also Al-
Albāni, *Sahīh Abu Dawud* 1/166, see invocation no. 37
above.

O Allāh, forgive me all my sins, great and small, the first and the last, those that are apparent and those that are hidden.[64]

◆

٤٧-«اللَّهُمَّ إِنِّي أَعُوذُ بِرِضَاكَ مِنْ سَخَطِكَ، وَبِمُعَافَاتِكَ مِنْ عُقُوبَتِكَ، وَأَعُوذُ بِكَ مِنْكَ، لَا أُحْصِي ثَنَاءً عَلَيْكَ أَنْتَ كَمَا أَثْنَيْتَ عَلَى نَفْسِكَ».

Allaahumma 'innee 'a'oothu biridhaaka min sakhatika, wa bimu'aafaatika min 'uqoo-batika wa 'a'oothu bika minka, laa 'uhsee thanaa'an 'alayka 'Anta kamaa 'athnayta 'alaa nafsika.

O Allāh, I seek protection in Your pleasure from Your anger, and I seek protection in Your forgiveness from Your punishment. I seek protection in You from You. I cannot count Your praises. You are as You have praised Yourself.[65]

---

64. Muslim 1/350.
65. Muslim 1/352

20. In between *Sujood*

٤٨ -«رَبِّ اغْفِرْ لِي رَبِّ اغْفِرْ لِي».

Rabbighfir lee, Rabbighfir lee.

My Lord, forgive me. My Lord, forgive me.[66]

---

٤٩ -«اللَّهُمَّ اغْفِرْ لِي، وَارْحَمْنِي، وَاهْدِنِي، وَاجْبُرْنِي،
وَعَافِنِي، وَارْزُقْنِي، وَارْفَعْنِي».

*Allaahum-maghfir lee, warhamnee, wahdinee,
wajburnee, wa ʿaafinee, warzuqnee, warfaʿnee.*

O Allāh forgive me, have mercy on me, guide
me, support me, protect me, provide for me
and elevate me.[67]

---

66. Abu Dawud 1/231. See also Al-Albāni, *Sahīh Ibn
    Mājah* 1/148.

67. Abu Dawud, Ibn Mājah, At-Tirmithi. See also Al-Albāni,
    Sahīh At-Tirmithi 1/90 and *Sahīh Ibn Mājah* 1/148.

21. During Qur'ānic *Sajda*

٥٠-"سَجَدَ وَجْهِيَ لِلَّذِي خَلَقَهُ، وَشَقَّ سَمْعَهُ وَبَصَرَهُ، بِحَوْلِهِ وَقُوَّتِهِ، فَتَبَارَكَ اللهُ أَحْسَنُ الْخَالِقِينَ".

Sajada wajhiya lillathee khalaqahu, wa shaqqa sam'ahu wa basarahu bihawlihi wa quwwati-hi. Fatabaarakallaahu 'ahsanul khaaliqeen.

I have prostrated my face to the One Who created it, and gave it hearing and sight by His might and His power. Glory is to Allāh, the Best of creators.[68]

◆

٥١-اللَّهُمَّ اكْتُبْ لِي بِهَا عِنْدَكَ أَجْرًا، وَضَعْ عَنِّي بِهَا وِزْرًا، وَاجْعَلْهَا لِي عِنْدَكَ ذُخْرًا، وَتَقَبَّلْهَا مِنِّي كَمَا تَقَبَّلْتَهَا مِنْ عَبْدِكَ دَاوُدَ"

Allaahum-maktub lee bihaa 'indaka 'ajran, wa dha' 'annee bihaa wizran, waj'alhaa lee 'inda-

_____

68. At-Tirmithi.i 2/474, Aḥmad 6/30, and Al-Ḥākim who graded it authentic and Aṯh-Thahabi agreed with him 1/220.

*ka thukhran, wa taqabbalhaa minnee kamaa
taqabbaltahaa min 'abdika Daawooda.*

O Allāh, write it as a reward for me, and
release me from a burden for it, and make it a
treasure for me in Paradise. Accept it from me
as You accepted it from your servant Dawud.[69]

---

22. During *At-Tashahhud*

٥٢-"التَّحِيَّاتُ لِلَّهِ، وَالصَّلَوَاتُ، وَالطَّيِّبَاتُ، السَّلَامُ
عَلَيْكَ أَيُّهَا النَّبِيُّ وَرَحْمَةُ اللهِ وَبَرَكَاتُهُ، السَّلَامُ عَلَيْنَا وَعَلَى
عِبَادِ اللهِ الصَّالِحِينَ. أَشْهَدُ أَنْ لَا إِلَهَ إِلَّا اللهُ وَأَشْهَدُ أَنَّ
مُحَمَّدًا عَبْدُهُ وَرَسُولُهُ".

*Attahiyyaatu lillaahi wassalawaatu, wattayy-
ibaatu, assalaamu 'alayka 'ayyuhan-Nabiyyu
wa rahmatullaahi wa barakaatuhu, assalaamu
'alaynaa wa 'alaa 'ibaadillaahis-saaliheen. 'Ash-
hadu 'an laa 'ilaaha 'illallaahu wa 'ash-hadu
'anna Muhammadan 'abduhu wa Rasooluhu.*

---

69. At-Tirmithi 2/473, and Al-Hākim who graded it
    authentic and Ath-Thahabi agreed 1/219.

All greetings of humility are for Allāh, and all prayers and goodness. Peace be upon you, O Prophet, and the mercy of Allāh and His blessings. Peace be upon us and upon the righteous slaves of Allāh. I bear witness that there is none worthy of worship but Allāh, and I bear witness that Muhammad is His slave and His Messenger.[70]

---

23. Sending Blessings on the Prophet ﷺ after the *Tashahhud*

٥٣- «اللَّهُمَّ صَلِّ عَلَى مُحَمَّدٍ وَعَلَى آلِ مُحَمَّدٍ، كَمَا صَلَّيْتَ عَلَى إِبْرَاهِيمَ وَعَلَى آلِ إِبْرَاهِيمَ، إِنَّكَ حَمِيدٌ مَجِيدٌ، اللَّهُمَّ بَارِكْ عَلَى مُحَمَّدٍ وَعَلَى آلِ مُحَمَّدٍ كَمَا بَارَكْتَ عَلَى إِبْرَاهِيمَ وَعَلَى آلِ إِبْرَاهِيمَ، إِنَّكَ حَمِيدٌ مَجِيدٌ» .

Allaahumma salli 'alaa Muhammadin wa 'alaa 'aali Muhammadin, kamaa sallayta 'alaa 'Ibraaheema wa 'alaa 'aali 'Ibraaheema, 'in-

---

70. Al-Bukhāri, Muslim 1/301. See also Al-Asqalāni, *Fathul-Bāri* 1/13.

*naka Hameedun Majeed. Allaahumma baarik
'alaa Muhammadin wa 'alaa 'aali Muhammadin, kamaa baarakta 'alaa 'Ibraaheema wa
'alaa 'aali 'Ibraaheema, 'innaka Hameedun
Majeed.*

O Allāh, bestow Your favour on Muhammad
and on the family of Muhammad as You have
bestowed Your favour on Ibrahim and on the
family of Ibrahim, You are Praiseworthy, Most
Glorious. O Allāh, bless Muhammad and the
family of Muhammad as You have blessed
Ibrahim and the family of Ibrahim, You are
Praiseworthy, Most Glorious.[71]

---•---

٥٤-«اللَّهُمَّ صَلِّ عَلَى مُحَمَّدٍ وَعَلَى أَزْوَاجِهِ وَذُرِّيَّتِهِ، كَمَا
صَلَّيْتَ عَلَى آلِ إِبْرَاهِيمَ، وَبَارِكْ عَلَى مُحَمَّدٍ وَعَلَى أَزْوَاجِهِ
وَذُرِّيَّتِهِ، كَمَا بَارَكْتَ عَلَى آلِ إِبْرَاهِيمَ، إِنَّكَ حَمِيدٌ مَجِيدٌ».

*Allaahumma salli 'alaa Muhammadin wa 'alaa
'azwaajihi wa <u>th</u>urriyyatihi, kamaa sallayta*

---

71. Al-Bukhari, cf. Al-Asqalāni, *Fathul-Bāri* 6/ 408.

'alaa 'aali 'Ibraaheema. Wa baarik 'alaa
Muhammadin wa 'alaa 'azwaajihi wa thurri-
yyatihi, kamaa baarakta 'alaa 'aali 'Ibraaheema. 'Innaka Hameedun Majeed.

O Allāh, bestow Your favour on Muhammad
and upon his wives and progeny as You have
bestowed Your favour upon the family of
Ibrahim. And bless Muhammad and his wives
and progeny as You have blessed the family of
Ibrahim, You are full of praise, Most Glorious.[72]

◆

24. After the final *Tashahhud* and before ending the prayer

٥٥-«اللَّهُمَّ إِنِّي أَعُوذُ بِكَ مِنْ عَذَابِ الْقَبْرِ، وَمِنْ عَذَابِ جَهَنَّمَ،
وَمِنْ فِتْنَةِ الْمَحْيَا وَالْمَمَاتِ، وَمِنْ شَرِّ فِتْنَةِ الْمَسِيحِ الدَّجَّالِ» .

*Allaahumma 'innee 'a'oothu bika min 'athaabil-
qabri, wa min 'athaabi jahannama, wa min
fitnatil-mahyaa walmamaati, wa min sharri
fitnatil-maseehid-dajjaal.*

---

72. Al-Bukhāri, from Al-Asqalāni, *Fathul-Bāri* 6/407,
    Muslim 1/306.

O Allāh, I seek refuge in You from the punishment of the grave, and from the punishment
of Hell-fire, and from the trials of life and
death, and from the evil of the trial of the False
Messiah.[73]

* * *

٥٦-«اللَّهُمَّ إِنِّي أَعُوذُ بِكَ مِنْ عَذَابِ الْقَبْرِ، وَأَعُوذُ بِكَ
مِنْ فِتْنَةِ الْمَسِيحِ الدَّجَّالِ، وَأَعُوذُ بِكَ مِنْ فِتْنَةِ الْمَحْيَا
وَالْمَمَاتِ. اللَّهُمَّ إِنِّي أَعُوذُ بِكَ مِنَ الْمَأْثَمِ وَالْمَغْرَمِ».

*Allaahumma 'innee 'a'oothu bika min 'athaab-
bil qabri, wa 'a'oothu bika minfitnatil ma-
seehid-dajjaali, wa 'a'oothu bika min fitnatil-
mahyaa walmamaati. Allaahumma 'innee
'a'oothu bika minal-ma'thami walmaghrami.*

O Allāh, I seek refuge in You from the punishment of the grave, and I seek refuge in You
from the trial of the False Messiah, and I seek
refuge in You from the trials of life and death.

---

73. Al-Bukhāri 2/102, Muslim 1/412, and this is Muslim's
   wording.

O Allāh, I seek refuge in You from sin and from debt.[74]

---◆---

٥٧-«اللّٰهُمَّ إِنِّي ظَلَمْتُ نَفْسِي ظُلْمًا كَثِيرًا، وَلَا يَغْفِرُ الذُّنُوبَ إِلَّا أَنْتَ، فَاغْفِرْلِي مَغْفِرَةً مِنْ عِنْدِكَ وَارْحَمْنِي إِنَّكَ أَنْتَ الْغَفُورُ الرَّحِيمُ».

Allaahumma 'innee dhalamtu nafsee dhulman katheeran, wa laa yaghfiruth-thunooba 'illaa 'Anta, faghfir lee maghfiratan min 'indika war-hamnee 'innaka 'Antal Ghafoorur-Raheem.

O Allāh, I have greatly wronged myself and no one forgives sins but You. So, grant me forgiveness and have mercy on me. Surely, You are Forgiving, Merciful.[75]

---◆---

74. Al-Bukhāri 1/202, Muslim 1/412.
75. Al-Bukhāri 8/168, Muslim 4/2078.

٥٨-«اللَّهُمَّ اغْفِرْ لِي مَا قَدَّمْتُ، وَمَا أَخَّرْتُ، وَمَا أَسْرَرْتُ، وَمَا أَعْلَنْتُ، وَمَا أَسْرَفْتُ، وَمَا أَنْتَ أَعْلَمُ بِهِ مِنِّي. أَنْتَ الْمُقَدِّمُ، وَأَنْتَ الْمُؤَخِّرُ لَا إِلَهَ إِلَّا أَنْتَ».

Allaahum-maghfir lee maa qaddamtu, wa maa 'akhkhartu, wa maa 'asrartu, wa maa 'a'lantu, wa maa 'asraftu, wa maa 'Anta 'a'lamu bihi minnee. 'Antal-Muqaddimu, wa 'Antal- Mu'akh- khiru laa 'ilaaha 'illaa 'Anta.

O Allāh, forgive me what I have sent before me and what I have left behind me, what I have concealed and what I have done openly, what I have done in excess, and what You are better aware of than I. You are the One Who sends forth and You are the One Who delays. There is none worthy of worship but You.[76]

---

76. Muslim 1/534.

٥٩-«اللَّهُمَّ أَعِنِّي عَلَى ذِكْرِكَ، وَشُكْرِكَ، وَحُسْنِ عِبَادَتِكَ».

Allaahumma 'a'innee 'alaa thikrika, wa shukrika, wa husni 'ibaadatika.

O Allāh, help me to remember You, to give You thanks, and to perform Your worship in the best manner.[77]

٦٠-«اللَّهُمَّ إِنِّي أَعُوذُ بِكَ مِنَ الْبُخْلِ، وَأَعُوذُ بِكَ مِنَ الْجُبْنِ، وَأَعُوذُ بِكَ مِنْ أَنْ أُرَدَّ إِلَى أَرْذَلِ الْعُمُرِ، وَأَعُوذُ بِكَ مِنْ فِتْنَةِ الدُّنْيَا وَعَذَابِ الْقَبْرِ».

Allaahumma 'innee 'a'oothu bika minal bukhli, wa a'oothu bika minal-jubni, wa a'oothu bika min 'an 'uradda 'ilaa 'arthalil-'umuri, wa a'oothu minfitnatid-dunyaa wa 'athaabil-qabri.

---

77. Abu Dawud 2/86, An-Nasā'i 3/53. See also Al-Albāni *Saḥīḥ Abu Dawud* 1/284.

O Allāh, I seek Your protection from miserliness, I seek Your protection from cowardice, and I seek Your protection from being returned to feeble old age. I seek Your protection from the trials of this world and from the torment of the grave.[78]

* * *

٦١-«اللَّهُمَّ إِنِّي أَسْأَلُكَ الْجَنَّةَ وَأَعُوذُ بِكَ مِنَ النَّارِ».

Allaahumma 'innee 'as'alu kal-janna ta wa 'a'oothu bika minan-naar.

O Allāh, I ask You for Paradise and seek Your protection from the Fire.[79]

* * *

٦٢-«اللَّهُمَّ بِعِلْمِكَ الْغَيْبَ وَقُدْرَتِكَ عَلَى الْخَلْقِ أَحْيِنِي مَا عَلِمْتَ الْحَيَاةَ خَيْرًا لِي وَتَوَفَّنِي إِذَا عَلِمْتَ الْوَفَاةَ خَيْرًا لِي، اللَّهُمَّ إِنِّي أَسْأَلُكَ خَشْيَتَكَ فِي الْغَيْبِ وَالشَّهَادَةِ، وَأَسْأَلُكَ

---

78. Al-Bukhāri, cf. Al-Asqalāni, *Fathul-Bāri* 6/35.

79. Abu Dawud. See also Al-Albani, *Sahīh Ibn Mājah* 2/328.

كَلِمَةَ الْحَقِّ فِي الرِّضَا وَالْغَضَبِ، وَأَسْأَلُكَ الْقَصْدَ فِي الْغِنَى وَالْفَقْرِ، وَأَسْأَلُكَ نَعِيمًا لَا يَنْفَدُ، وَأَسْأَلُكَ قُرَّةَ عَيْنٍ لَا تَنْقَطِعُ، وَأَسْأَلُكَ الرِّضَا بَعْدَ الْقَضَاءِ، وَأَسْأَلُكَ بَرْدَ الْعَيْشِ بَعْدَ الْمَوْتِ، وَأَسْأَلُكَ لَذَّةَ النَّظَرِ إِلَى وَجْهِكَ وَالشَّوْقَ إِلَى لِقَائِكَ فِي غَيْرِ ضَرَّاءَ مُضِرَّةٍ وَلَا فِتْنَةٍ مُضِلَّةٍ، اللَّهُمَّ زَيِّنَّا بِزِينَةِ الْإِيمَانِ وَاجْعَلْنَا هُدَاةً مُهْتَدِينَ».

*Allaahumma bi'ilmikal-ghayba wa qudrati-
ka 'alal-khalqi 'ahyinee maa 'alimtal hayaata
khayran lee wa tawaffanee 'ithaa 'alimtal-wa-
faata khayran lee, Allaahumma 'innee 'as.alu-
ka khashyataka fil-ghaybi wash-shahaadati,
wa 'as.aluka kalimatal haqqi fir-ridhaa
walghadhabi, wa 'as.alukal qasda fil-ghinaa
walfaqri, wa 'as.aluka na'eeman laa yanfadu,
wa 'as.aluka qurrata 'aynin laa tanqati'u, wa
'as.alukar-ridhaa ba'dal-qadhaa'i, wa 'as.alu-
ka bardal-'ayshi ba'dal-mawti, wa 'as.aluka
laththatan nadhari 'ilaa wajhika wash-shawqa
'ilaa liqaa 'ika fee ghayri dharraa'a mudhirra-
tin wa laa fitnatin mudhillatin, Allaahumma
zayyinnaa bizeenatil-'eemaani waj'alnaa
hudaatan muhtadeen.*

O Allāh, by Your Knowledge of the unseen and by Your Power over creation, let me live if You know that life is good for me, and let me die if You know that death is good for me. O Allāh, I ask You to grant me fear of You in private and in public. I ask you for the word of truth in times of contentment and anger. I ask You for moderation in wealth and in poverty. I ask you for blessings never ceasing and the coolness of my eye (i.e. pleasure) that never ends. I ask You for pleasure after Your Judgment and I ask You for a life of coolness after death. I ask You for the delight of gazing upon Your Face and the joy of meeting You without any harm and misleading trials befalling me. O Allāh, dress us with the beauty of Faith, and make us guides who are upon (correct) guidance.[80]

---

80. An-Nasā'i 3/54, 55, Aḥmad 4/364. See also Al-Albāni, *Sahīh An-Nasā'i* 1/281.

٦٣-«اللَّهُمَّ إِنِّي أَسْأَلُكَ يَا اللهُ بِأَنَّكَ الْوَاحِدُ الْأَحَدُ الصَّمَدُ الَّذِي لَمْ يَلِدْ وَلَمْ يُولَدْ وَلَمْ يَكُنْ لَهُ كُفُوًا أَحَدٌ، أَنْ تَغْفِرَ لِي ذُنُوبِي إِنَّكَ أَنْتَ الْغَفُورُ الرَّحِيمُ».

63. Allaahumma 'innee 'as'aluka yaa Allaahu
bi 'annakal-Waahidul-'Ahadus-Samadul lathee,
lam yalid wa lam yoolad, wa lam yakun lahu
kufuwan 'Ahad, 'an taghfira lee thunoobee
'innaka 'Antal-Ghafoorur-Raheem.

O Allāh, I ask You. O Allāh, You are the One,
the Only, Self-Sufficient Master, Who was not
begotten and begets not and none is equal to
Him. Forgive me my sins, surely you are Forgiving, Merciful.[81]

--------- • ---------

---

81. An-Nasā'i 3/52, Aḥmad 4/338. See also Al-Albāni,
   Sahīh An-Nasā'i 1/280 and Sifat Salātun-Nabi, p. 204.

٦٤-"اللَّهُمَّ إِنِّي أَسْأَلُكَ بِأَنَّ لَكَ الْحَمْدَ لَا إِلَهَ إِلَّا أَنْتَ وَحْدَكَ لَا شَرِيكَ لَكَ، الْمَنَّانُ، يَا بَدِيعَ السَّمَوَاتِ وَالْأَرْضِ يَا ذَا الْجَلَالِ وَالْإِكْرَامِ، يَاحَيُّ يَاقَيُّومُ إِنِّي أَسْأَلُكَ الْجَنَّةَ وَأَعُوذُ بِكَ مِنَ النَّارِ".

64. Allaahumma 'innee 'as'aluka bi'anna lakal-hamda laa 'ilaaha 'illaa 'Anta wahdaka laa shareeka laka, Al-Mannaanu, yaa Badee 'as-samaawaati wal'ardhi yaa Thal-Jalaali wal-'Ikraam, yaa Hayyu yaa Qayyoomu 'innee 'as'alukal-jannata wa 'a'oothu bika minan-naar.

O Allāh, I ask You, as You are the Owner of praise, there is none worthy of worship but You alone, You have no partner. You are the Giver of all good. O Creator of the heavens and the earth, Owner of majesty and honor. O Living and Everlasting One, I ask you for Paradise and I seek refuge in You from the Fire.[82]

---

82. Abu Dawud, An-Nasā'i, Ibn Mājah, At-Tirmithi. See also Al-Albāni, *Sahīh ibn Mājah* 2/329.

٦٥-«اللَّهُمَّ إِنِّي أَسْأَلُكَ بِأَنِّي أَشْهَدُ أَنَّكَ أَنْتَ اللهُ لَا إِلَهَ
إِلَّا أَنْتَ الْأَحَدُ الصَّمَدُ الَّذِي لَمْ يَلِدْ وَلَمْ يُولَدْ وَلَمْ يَكُنْ لَهُ
كُفُوًا أَحَدٌ».

Allaahumma 'innee 'as'aluka bi'annee 'ash-hadu 'annaka 'Antallaahu laa 'ilaaha 'illaa 'Antal-'Ahadus-Samadul-lathee lam yalid wa lam yoolad wa lam yakun lahu kufuwan 'Ahad.

O Allāh, I ask You, by the fact that I bear witness that You are Allāh. There is none worthy of worship but You, the Only God, Independent of creation, Who was not begotten and begets not, and none is equal to Him. [83]

---

83. Abu Dawud 2/62, Ibn Mājah 2/1267, At-Tirmithi 5/515, Aḥmad 5/360. See also Al Albani, *Sahīh Ibn Mājah* 2/329 and *Sahīh At-Tirmithi* 3/163.

25. After completing the *Salat*

٦٦-«أَسْتَغْفِرُ اللهَ (ثَلَاثًا) اللَّهُمَّ أَنْتَ السَّلَامُ وَمِنْكَ
السَّلَامُ، تَبَارَكْتَ يَا ذَا الْجَلَالِ وَالْإِكْرَامِ».

'Astaghfirullaaha Allaahumma 'Antas Salaamu
wa minkas-salaamu, tabaarakta yaa <u>Th</u>al-Jalaa-
li wal-'Ikraam.

I seek the forgiveness of Allāh (three times).
O Allāh, You are Peace and from You comes
peace. Blessed are You, O Owner of majesty
and honor.[84]

------- ♦ -------

٦٧-«لَا إِلٰهَ إِلَّا اللهُ وَحْدَهُ لَا شَرِيكَ لَهُ، لَهُ الْمُلْكُ وَلَهُ الْحَمْدُ
وَهُوَ عَلَى كُلِّ شَيْءٍ قَدِيرٌ، اللَّهُمَّ لَا مَانِعَ لِمَا أَعْطَيْتَ، وَلَا
مُعْطِيَ لِمَا مَنَعْتَ، وَلَا يَنْفَعُ ذَا الْجَدِّ مِنْكَ الْجَدُّ».

Laa 'ilaaha 'illallaahu wahdahu laa shareeka
lahu, lahul-mulku wa lahul-hamdu wa Huwa
'alaa kulli shay'in Qadeer, Allaahumma laa
maani'a limaa 'a'tayta, wa laa mu'tiya limaa
mana'ta, wa laa yanfa'u <u>th</u>al-jaddi minkal-jadd.

------

84. Muslim 1/414

None has the right to be worshipped but Allāh alone, He has no partner, His is the dominion and His is the praise, and He is Able to do all things. O Allāh, there is none who can withhold what You give, and none may give what You have withheld; and the might of the mighty person cannot benefit him against You.[85]

◆

٦٨-«لَا إِلَهَ إِلَّا اللهُ وَحْدَهُ لَا شَرِيكَ لَهُ، لَهُ الْمُلْكُ وَلَهُ الْحَمْدُ وَهُوَ عَلَى كُلِّ شَيْءٍ قَدِيرٌ، لَا حَوْلَ وَلَا قُوَّةَ إِلَّا بِاللهِ، لَا إِلَهَ إِلَّا اللهُ، وَلَا نَعْبُدُ إِلَّا إِيَّاهُ، لَهُ النِّعْمَةُ وَلَهُ الْفَضْلُ وَلَهُ الثَّنَاءُ الْحَسَنُ، لَا إِلَهَ إِلَّا اللهُ مُخْلِصِينَ لَهُ الدِّينَ وَلَوْ كَرِهَ الْكَافِرُونَ».

La 'ilaaha 'illallaahu wahdahu laa shareeka lahu, lahul-mulku, wa lahul-hamdu wa Huwa 'alaa kulli shay'in Qadeer. Laa hawla wa laa quwwata 'illaa billaahi, laa 'ilaaha 'illallaahu, wa laa na'budu 'illaa 'iyyaahu, lahun-ni'matu wa lahul-fadhlu wa lahuth-thanaa 'ul-hasanu, laa 'ilaaha 'illallaahu mukhliseena lahud-deena wa law karihal-kaafiroon.

---

85. Al-Bukhāri 1/255, Muslim 1/414.

None has the right to be worshipped but Allāh alone, He has no partner, His is the dominion and His is the praise and He is Able to do all things. There is no power and no might except by Allāh. None has the right to be worshipped but Allāh, and we do not worship any other besides Him. His is grace, and His is bounty and to Him belongs the most excellent praise. None has the right to be worshipped but Allāh. (We are) sincere in making our religious devotion to Him, even though the disbelievers may dislike it.[86]

---- • ----

٦٩-«سُبْحَانَ اللهِ، وَالْحَمْدُ للهِ، وَاللهُ أَكْبَرُ (ثَلَاثًا وَثَلَاثِينَ)
لَا إِلٰهَ إِلَّا اللهُ وَحْدَهُ لَا شَرِيكَ لَهُ، لَهُ الْمُلْكُ وَلَهُ الْحَمْدُ
وَهُوَ عَلَى كُلِّ شَيْءٍ قَدِيرٌ».

Subhaanallaahi, walhamdu lillaahi wallaahu 'Akbar, – Laa 'ilaaha 'illallaahu wahdahu laa shareeka lahu, lahul-mulku wa lahul-hamdu wa Huwa 'alaa kulli shay'in Qadeer.

---

86. Muslim 1/415.

Glory is to Allāh, and praise is to Allāh, and Allāh is the Most Great (say each thirty-three times). None has the right to be worshipped but Allāh alone, He has no partner, His is the dominion and His is the praise and He is Able to do all things.[87]

* * *

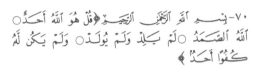

Bismillaahir-Rahmaanir-Raheem. Qul Huwal-laahu 'Ahad. Allaahus-Samad. Lam yalid wa lam yoolad. Wa lam yakun lahu kufuwan 'ahad.

With the Name of Allāh, the Most Gracious, the Most Merciful. Say: He is Allāh (the) One. The Self-Sufficient Master, Whom all creatures need, He begets not nor was He begotten, and there is none equal to Him.[88]

---

87. Muslim 1/418, Whoever says this after every prayer will be forgiven his sins even though they be as the foam of the sea.

88. *Al-Ikhlas* 112:1-4.

بِسْمِ اللَّهِ الرَّحْمَٰنِ الرَّحِيمِ ﴿قُلْ أَعُوذُ بِرَبِّ الْفَلَقِ ۝ مِن شَرِّ مَا خَلَقَ ۝ وَمِن شَرِّ غَاسِقٍ إِذَا وَقَبَ ۝ وَمِن شَرِّ النَّفَّاثَاتِ فِي الْعُقَدِ ۝ وَمِن شَرِّ حَاسِدٍ إِذَا حَسَدَ ﴾

Bismillaahir-Rahmaanir-Raheem.
Qul 'a'oothu birabbil-falaq. Min sharri maa khalaq. Wamin sharri ghaasiqin 'ithaa waqab. Wa min sharrin-naffaathaati fil 'uqad. Wa min sharri haasidin 'ithaa hasad.

With the Name of Allāh, the Most Gracious the Most Merciful. Say: I seek refuge with (Allāh) the Lord of the daybreak, from the evil of what He has created, and from the evil of the darkening (night) as it comes with its darkness, and from the evil of those who practice witchcraft when they blow in the knots, and from the evil of the envier when he envies.[89]

◆

---

89. *Al-Falaq* 113 :1-5.

بِسْمِ ٱللَّهِ ٱلرَّحْمَٰنِ ٱلرَّحِيمِ ﴿قُلْ أَعُوذُ بِرَبِّ ٱلنَّاسِ ٠ مَلِكِ ٱلنَّاسِ ٠ إِلَٰهِ ٱلنَّاسِ ٠ مِن شَرِّ ٱلْوَسْوَاسِ ٱلْخَنَّاسِ ٠ ٱلَّذِي يُوَسْوِسُ فِي صُدُورِ ٱلنَّاسِ ٠ مِنَ ٱلْجِنَّةِ وَٱلنَّاسِ﴾ .

Bismillaahir-Rahmaanir-Raheem.
Qul 'a'oodhu birabbin-naas. Malikin-naas.
'Ilaahin-naas. Min sharril-waswaasil-khannaas.
Allathee yuwaswisu fee sudoorin naas. Minal-jinnati wannaas.

With the Name of Allāh, the Most Gracious, the Most Merciful.
Say: I seek refuge with (Allāh) the Lord of mankind, the King of mankind, the God of mankind, from the evil of the whisperer who withdraws, who whispers in the breasts of mankind, of jinns and men.[90]
(These *Surahs* should be recited in Arabic after each prayer. After the *Maghrib* and *Fajr* prayers they should be recited three times each.)[91]

---

90. *An-Nas* 114 :1-6.
91. Abu Dawud 2/86, An-Nasā'i 3/68. See also Al-Albāni, *Sahīh At-Tirmithi* 2/8.

٧١- ﴿اللَّهُ لَا إِلَهَ إِلَّا هُوَ الْحَيُّ الْقَيُّومُ لَا تَأْخُذُهُ سِنَةٌ وَلَا نَوْمٌ لَهُ مَا فِي السَّمَوَاتِ وَمَا فِي الْأَرْضِ مَن ذَا الَّذِي يَشْفَعُ عِندَهُ إِلَّا بِإِذْنِهِ يَعْلَمُ مَا بَيْنَ أَيْدِيهِمْ وَمَا خَلْفَهُمْ وَلَا يُحِيطُونَ بِشَيْءٍ مِنْ عِلْمِهِ إِلَّا بِمَا شَاءَ وَسِعَ كُرْسِيُّهُ السَّمَوَاتِ وَالْأَرْضَ وَلَا يَؤُودُهُ حِفْظُهُمَا وَهُوَ الْعَلِيُّ الْعَظِيمُ﴾.

*Allaahu laa 'ilaaha 'illaa Huwal-Hayyul
Qayyoom, laa ta'khuthuhu sinatun wa laa
nawm, lahu maa fis-samaawaati wa maa
fil'ardh, man thal-lathee yashfa'u 'indahu
'illaa bi'ithnih, ya'lamu maa bayna 'aydee-
him wa maa khalfahum, wa laa yuheetoona
bishay'im-min 'ilmihi 'illaa bimaa shaa'a,
wasi'a kursiyyuhus-samaa- waati wal'ardh,
wa laa ya'ooduhu hifdhuhumaa, wa Huwal
'Aliyyul-'Adheem.*

Allāh! There is none worthy of worship but
He, the Ever Living, the One Who sustains and
protects all that exists. Neither slumber nor
sleep overtakes Him. To Him belongs whatever
is in the heavens and whatever is on the earth.
Who is he that can intercede with Him except

with His Permission? He knows what happens
to them in this world, and what will happen
to them in the Hereafter. And they will never
compass anything of His Knowledge except
that which He wills. His Throne extends over
the heavens and the earth, and He feels no
fatigue in guarding and preserving them. And
He is the Most High, the Most Great. (Recite
in Arabic after each prayer.)[92]

◆

٧٢-«لَا إِلَهَ إِلَّا اللهُ وَحْدَهُ لَا شَرِيكَ لَهُ، لَهُ الْمُلْكُ وَلَهُ
الْحَمْدُ يُحْيِي وَيُمِيتُ، وَهُوَ عَلَى كُلِّ شَيْءٍ قَدِيرٌ».

*Laa 'ilaaha 'illallaahu wahdahu laa shareeka
lahu, lahul-mulku wa lahul-hamdu yuhyee wa
yumeetu wa Huwa 'alaa kulli shay'in Qadeer.*

None has the right to be worshipped but
Allāh alone, Who has no partner. His is the

---

92. An-Nasā'i, *'Amalul-Yawmwal-Laylah* (Hadith no.100),
also Ibn As-Sunni (no. 121). See also Al-Albāni,
Sahīhul-Jami' As-Saghīr 5/339 and *Silsilatul-Ahādith
As-Sahīhah* 2/697 (no. 972).

dominion and His is the praise. He brings life and He causes death, and He is Able to do all things. (Recite ten times in Arabic after the *Maghrib* and *Fajr* prayers.)[93]

٧٣-«اللَّهُمَّ إِنِّي أَسْأَلُكَ عِلْمًا نَافِعًا، وَرِزْقًا طَيِّبًا، وَعَمَلًا مُتَقَبَّلًا».

Allaahumma 'innee 'as'aluka 'ilman naafi'an, wa rizqan tayyiban, wa 'amalan mutaqabbalan.

O Allāh, I ask You for knowledge that is of benefit, a good provision, and deeds that will be accepted. (Recite in Arabic after the Fajr prayer.)[94]

---

93. At-Tirmithi 5/515, Aḥmad 4/227. See its checking in Ibn Al-Qayyim Al-Jawziyyah's *Zādul Ma'ād* 1/300.

94. Ibn Mājah and others. See Al-Albani, *Sahīh Ibn Mājah* 1/152 and *Majma'uz-Zawā'id* 10/111.

26. *Istikhārah* (seeking Allāh's Counsel)

Jābir bin Abdullah ﷺ said: The Prophet ﷺ
used to teach us to seek Allāh's Counsel
in all matters, as he used to teach us a *Surah*
from the Qur'ān. He would say: When anyone
of you has an important matter to decide, let
him pray two *Rak'ahs* other than the obligato-
ry prayer, and then say:

٧٤-«اللّٰهُمَّ إِنِّي أَسْتَخِيرُكَ بِعِلْمِكَ، وَأَسْتَقْدِرُكَ بِقُدْرَتِكَ،
وَأَسْأَلُكَ مِنْ فَضْلِكَ الْعَظِيمِ، فَإِنَّكَ تَقْدِرُ وَلَا أَقْدِرُ،
وَتَعْلَمُ، وَلَا أَعْلَمُ، وَأَنْتَ عَلَّامُ الْغُيُوبِ، اللّٰهُمَّ إِنْ كُنْتَ
تَعْلَمُ أَنَّ هَذَا الْأَمْرَ- خَيْرٌ لِي فِي دِينِي وَمَعَاشِي وَعَاقِبَةِ
أَمْرِي- عَاجِلِهِ وَآجِلِهِ- فَاقْدُرْهُ لِي وَيَسِّرْهُ لِي ثُمَّ بَارِكْ لِي
فِيهِ، وَإِنْ كُنْتَ تَعْلَمُ أَنَّ هَذَا الْأَمْرَ شَرٌّ لِي فِي دِينِي
وَمَعَاشِي وَعَاقِبَةِ أَمْرِي - عَاجِلِهِ وَآجِلِهِ- فَاصْرِفْهُ عَنِّي
وَاصْرِفْنِي عَنْهُ وَاقْدُرْ لِيَ الْخَيْرَ حَيْثُ كَانَ ثُمَّ أَرْضِنِي بِهِ».

Allaahumma 'innee 'astakheeruka bi'ilmika,
wa 'astaqdiruka biqudratika, wa 'as'aluka
min fadhlikal-'Adheemi, fa'innaka taqdiru wa

*laa 'aqdiru, wa ta'lamu, wa laa 'a'lamu, wa
'Anta 'Allaamul-Ghuyoobi, Allaahumma 'in
kunta ta'lamu 'anna haathal- 'amra –* [then
mention the thing to be decided] *Khayrun lee
fee deenee wa ma'aashee wa 'aaqibati 'amree –*
[or say] *'Aajilihi wa 'aajilihi – Faqdurhu lee wa
yassirhu lee thumma baarik lee feehi, wa 'in
kunta ta'lamu 'anna haathal-'amra sharrun lee
fee deenee wa ma'aashee wa 'aaqibati 'amree –*
[or say] *'Aajilihi wa 'aajilihi – Fasrifhu 'annee
wasrifnee 'anhu waqdur liyal-khayra haythu
kaana thumma 'ardhinee bihi.*

O Allāh, I seek the counsel of Your Knowledge,
and I seek the help of Your Omnipotence, and
I beseech You for Your Magnificent Grace.
Surely, You are Capable and I am not. You
know and I know not, and You are the Knower of the unseen. O Allāh, if You know that
this matter [then mention the thing to be de-
cided] is good for me in my religion and in my
life and for my welfare in the life to come, – [or
say: in this life and the afterlife] – then ordain
it for me and make it easy for me, then bless

me in it. And if You know that this matter is bad for me in my religion and in my life and for my welfare in the life to come, – [or say: in this life and the afterlife] – then distance it from me, and distance me from it, and ordain for me what is good wherever it may be, and help me to be content with it.[95]

Whoever seeks the counsel of the Creator will not regret it and whoever seeks the advice of the believers will feel confident about his decisions. Allāh said in the Qur'ān:

﴿وَشَاوِرْهُمْ فِى ٱلْأَمْرِ فَإِذَا عَزَمْتَ فَتَوَكَّلْ عَلَى ٱللَّهِ﴾

"And consult them in the affair. Then when you have taken a decision, put your trust in Allāh."[96]

⋯⋯⋯ ◆ ⋯⋯⋯

---

95. Al-Bukhāri 7/162.

96. Aal-'Imrān 3:159.

27. Words of remembrance during morning and evening

All praise is due to Allāh alone, and peace and blessings be upon him after whom there is no other Prophet.[97]

٧٥- أَعُوذُ بِاللهِ مِنَ الشَّيْطَانِ الرَّجِيمِ ﴿ٱللهُ لَآ إِلَٰهَ إِلَّا هُوَ الْحَيُّ الْقَيُّومُ لَا تَأْخُذُهُ سِنَةٌ وَلَا نَوْمٌ لَّهُ مَا فِي السَّمَٰوَٰتِ وَمَا فِي الْأَرْضِ مَن ذَا الَّذِي يَشْفَعُ عِندَهُ إِلَّا بِإِذْنِهِ يَعْلَمُ مَا بَيْنَ أَيْدِيهِمْ وَمَا خَلْفَهُمْ وَلَا يُحِيطُونَ بِشَيْءٍ مِّنْ عِلْمِهِ إِلَّا بِمَا شَآءَ وَسِعَ كُرْسِيُّهُ السَّمَٰوَٰتِ وَالْأَرْضَ وَلَا يَؤُودُهُ حِفْظُهُمَا وَهُوَ الْعَلِيُّ الْعَظِيمُ﴾

'A'oothu billaahi minash-Shaytaanir rajeem. Allaahu laa 'ilaaha 'illa Huwal Hayyul-

---

97. Anas ﷺ said that he heard the Prophet ﷺ say: "That I sit with people remembering Almighty Allāh from the morning (*Fajr*) prayer until sunrise is more beloved to me than freeing four slaves from among the Children of Isma'il. That I sit with people remembering Allāh from the afternoon ('*Asr*) prayer until the sun sets is more beloved to me than freeing four slaves from among the Children of Isma'il." This was reported by Abu Dawud (no. 3667). Al-Albāni graded it good in *Sahīh Abu Dawud* 2/698.

Qayyoom, laa ta'khu__thu__hu sinatun wa laa nawm, lahu maa fis-samaawaati wa maa fil-'ardh, man __th__al-la__th__ee yashfa'u 'indahu 'illaa bi'i__th__nih, ya'lamu maa bayna 'aydee-him wa maa khalfahum, wa laa yuheetoona bishay'im-min 'ilmihi 'illaa bimaa shaa'a, wasi'a kursiyyuhus samaawaati wal'ardh, wa laa ya'ooduhu hif__dh__uhumaa, wa Huwal-'Ali-yyul-'A__dh__eem.

I seek refuge in Allāh from Satan the outcast. – Allāh! There is none worthy of worship but He, the Ever Living, the One Who sustains and protects all that exists. Neither slumber nor sleep overtakes Him. To Him belongs whatever is in the heavens and whatever is on the earth. Who is he that can intercede with Him except with His Permission? He knows what happens to them in this world, and what will happen to them in the Hereafter. And they will never encompass anything of His Knowledge except that which He wills. His Throne extends over the heavens and the earth, and He feels no fatigue in guarding and preserving them. And He is the Most High, the Most Great.[98]

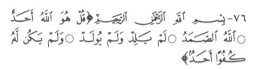

Bismillaahir-Rahmaanir-Raheem.
Qul Huwallahu 'Ahad. Allaahus-Samad.
Lam yalid wa lam yoolad. Wa lam yakun lahu
kufuwan 'ahad.

With the Name of Allāh, the Most Gracious, the Most Merciful. Say: He is Allāh (the) One. The Self-Sufficient Master, Whom all creatures need, He begets not nor was He begotten, and there is none equal to Him.

---

98. Whoever says this when he rises in the morning will be protected from jinns until he retires in the evening, and whoever says it when retiring in the evening will be protected from the jinns until he rises in the morning. It was reported by Al-Hākim 1/562. Al-Albāni graded it as authentic in *Sahīhut-Targhīb wat-Tarhīb* 1/273, and traces it to An-Nasā'i and At-Tabarāni. He says that At-Tabarāni's chain of transmission is reliable (*Jayyid*).

بِسْمِ اللَّهِ الرَّحْمَنِ الرَّحِيمِ ﴿قُلْ أَعُوذُ بِرَبِّ الْفَلَقِ ٥ مِن شَرِّ مَا خَلَقَ ٥ وَمِن شَرِّ غَاسِقٍ إِذَا وَقَبَ ٥ وَمِن شَرِّ النَّفَّثَتِ فِي الْعُقَدِ ٥وَمِن شَرِّ حَاسِدٍ إِذَا حَسَدَ ﴾

Bismillaahir-Rahmaanir-Raheem.
Qul 'a'oothu birabbil-falaq. Min sharri ma khalaq. Wa min sharri ghaasiqin 'ithaa waqab. Wa min sharrin-naffaathaati fil-'uqad. Wa min sharri haasidin 'ithaa hasad.

With the Name of Allāh, the Most Gracious, the Most Merciful. Say: I seek refuge with (Allāh) the Lord of the daybreak, from the evil of what He has created, and from the evil of the darkening (night) as it comes with its darkness, and from the evil of those who practice witchcraft when they blow in the knots, and from the evil of the envier when he envies.

---◆---

بِسْمِ اللَّهِ الرَّحْمَٰنِ الرَّحِيمِ ﴿قُلْ أَعُوذُ بِرَبِّ النَّاسِ ٠ مَلِكِ النَّاسِ ٠ إِلَٰهِ النَّاسِ ٠ مِن شَرِّ الْوَسْوَاسِ الْخَنَّاسِ ٠ الَّذِي يُوَسْوِسُ فِي صُدُورِ النَّاسِ ٠ مِنَ الْجِنَّةِ وَالنَّاسِ﴾ .

Bismillaahir-Rahmaanir-Raheem.
Qul 'a'oothu birabbin-naas. Malikin-naas.
'Ilaahin-naas. Min sharril-waswaasil khannaas.
Allathee yuwaswisu fee sudoorin naas. Minal-
jinnati wannaas.

With the Name of Allāh, the Most Gracious,
theMost Merciful. Say: I seek refuge with
(Allāh) the Lord of mankind, the King of mankind, the God of mankind, from the evil of the
whisperer who withdraws, Who whispers in
the breasts of mankind, of jinns and men.
(Recite these three times each in Arabic.)[99]

---

99. Whoever recites these three times in the morning and
   in the evening, they will suffice him (as a protection)
   against everything. The Hadith was reported by Abu
   Dawud 4/322, and At-Tirmithi 5/567. See Al-Albāni's
   Sahīh At-Tirmithi 3/182.

٧٧-«أَصْبَحْنَا وَأَصْبَحَ الْمُلْكُ لله وَالْحَمْدُ لله، لَا إِلَهَ إِلَّا
اللهُ وَحْدَهُ لَا شَرِيكَ لَهُ، لَهُ الْمُلْكُ وَلَهُ الْحَمْدُ وَهُوَ عَلَى
كُلِّ شَيْءٍ قَدِيرٌ، رَبِّ أَسْأَلُكَ خَيْرَ مَا فِي هَذَا الْيَوْمِ وَخَيْرَ
مَا بَعْدَهُ، وَأَعُوذُ بِكَ مِنْ شَرِّ مَا فِي هَذَا الْيَوْمِ وَشَرِّ مَا
بَعْدَهُ، رَبِّ أَعُوذُ بِكَ مِنَ الْكَسَلِ، وَسُوءِ الْكِبَرِ، رَبِّ
أَعُوذُ بِكَ مِنْ عَذَابٍ فِي النَّارِ وَعَذَابٍ فِي الْقَبْرِ».

'Asbahnaa wa 'asbahal-mulku lillaahi walhamdu lillaahi, laa 'ilaaha 'illallaahu wahdahu
laa shareeka lahu, lahul-mulku wa lahul-hamdu wa Huwa 'alaa kulli shay'in Qadeer. Rabbi
'as'aluka khayra maa fee haatẖal-yawmi wa
khayra maa ba'dahu wa 'a'ootẖu bika min
sharri maa fee haatẖal-yawmi wa sharri maa
ba'dahu, Rabbi 'a'ootẖu bika minal-kasali, wa
soo'il-kibāri, Rabbi 'a'ootẖu bika min
'atẖaabin fin-naari wa 'atẖaabin fil-qabri.

We have entered a new day[100] and with it all dominion is Allāh's. Praise is to Allāh. None has the right to be worshipped but Allāh alone, Who has no partner. To Allāh belongs the dominion, and to Him is the praise and He is Able to do all things. My Lord, I ask You for the goodness of this day and of the days that come after it, and I seek refuge in You from the evil of this day and of the days that come after it.[101] My Lord, I seek refuge in You from laziness and helpless old age. My Lord, I seek refuge in You from the punishment of Hell fire, and from the punishment of the grave.[102]

---------------- ◆ ----------------

100. When you say this in the evening you should say *'Amsaynaa wa'amsal-mulku lillaah* (We have ended another day and with it all dominion is Allāh's.)

101. When you say this in the evening you should say: *Rabbi 'as'aluka khayra maa fee haathihil-laylati, wa khayra maa ba'dahaa, wa 'a'oothu bika min sharri maa fee haathihil-laylati wa sharri maa ba'dahaa:* "I ask You for the good things of this night and of the nights that come after it and I seek refuge in You from the evil of this night and of the nights that come after it."

102. Muslim 4/2088.

٧٨-«اللَّهُمَّ بِكَ أَصْبَحْنَا، وَبِكَ أَمْسَيْنَا، وَبِكَ نَحْيَا، وَبِكَ نَمُوتُ وَإِلَيْكَ النُّشُورُ».

Allaahumma bika 'asbahnaa, wa bika 'amsay-naa, wa bika nahyaa, wa bika namootu wa 'ilaykan-nushoor.

O Allāh, by You we enter the morning and by You we enter the evening,[103] by You we live and and by You we die, and to You is the Final Return.[104]

◆

٧٩-«اللَّهُمَّ أَنْتَ رَبِّي لَا إِلَهَ إِلَّا أَنْتَ، خَلَقْتَنِي وَأَنَا عَبْدُكَ، وَأَنَا عَلَى عَهْدِكَ وَوَعْدِكَ مَا اسْتَطَعْتُ، أَعُوذُ بِكَ مِنْ شَرِّ مَا صَنَعْتُ، أَبُوءُ لَكَ بِنِعْمَتِكَ عَلَيَّ، وَأَبُوءُ بِذَنْبِي فَاغْفِرْ لِي فَإِنَّهُ لَا يَغْفِرُ الذُّنُوبَ إِلَّا أَنْتَ».

---

103. When you say this in the evening you should say:
Allaahumma bika 'amsaynaa wa bika 'asbahnaa, wa bika nahyaa, wa bika namoot, wa 'ilaykal-maseer:
"O Allāh, You bring us the end of the day as You bring us its beginning, You bring us life and you bring us death, and to You is our fate."

104. *Sahīh At-Tirmithi* 3/142.

Allaahumma 'Anta Rabbee laa 'ilaaha 'illaa 'Anta, khalaqtanee wa 'anaa 'abduka, wa 'anaa 'alaa 'ahdika wa wa'dika mastata'tu, 'a'oothu bika min sharri maa sana'tu, 'aboo'u laka bini'matika 'alayya, wa 'aboo'u bithanbee faghfir lee fa'innahu laa yaghfiruth thunooba 'illaa 'Anta.

O Allāh, You are my Lord, there is none worthy of worship but You. You created me and I am your slave. I keep Your covenant, and my pledge to You so far as I am able. I seek refuge in You from the evil of what I have done. I admit to Your blessings upon me, and I admit to my misdeeds. Forgive me, for there is none who may forgive sins but You.[105]

---

105. Whoever recites this with conviction in the evening and dies during that night shall enter Paradise, and whoever recites it with conviction in the morning and dies during that day shall enter Paradise, Al-Bukhāri 7/150. Other reports are in *An-Nasā'i* and *At-Tirmithi*.

٨٠-«اللَّهُمَّ إِنِّي أَصْبَحْتُ أُشْهِدُكَ وَأُشْهِدُ حَمَلَةَ عَرْشِكَ،
وَمَلَائِكَتَكَ وَجَمِيعَ خَلْقِكَ، أَنَّكَ أَنْتَ اللهُ لَا إِلَهَ إِلَّا أَنْتَ
وَحْدَكَ لَا شَرِيكَ لَكَ، وَأَنَّ مُحَمَّدًا عَبْدُكَ وَرَسُولُكَ».

*Allaahumma 'innee 'asbahtu 'ush-hiduka wa
'ush-hidu hamalata 'arshika, wa malaa'ikataka
wajamee'a khalqika, 'annaka 'Antallaahu laa
'ilaaha 'illaa 'Anta wahdaka laa shareeka laka,
wa 'anna Muhammadan 'abduka wa Rasooluka.*

O Allāh, I have entered a new morning[106] and
call upon You and upon the bearers of Your
Throne, upon Your angels and all creation to
bear witness that surely You are Allāh, there is
none worthy of worship but You alone, You
have no partners, and that Muhammad is Your
slave and Your Messenger. (Recite the above
four times in Arabic.)[107]

---

106. When you say this in the evening you should say,
Allaahumma 'innee 'amsaytu… : "O Allāh, I have
ended another day…"

107. "Allāh will spare whoever says this four times in
the morning or evening from the fire of Hell," Abu
Dawud 4/317. It was also reported by Al-Bukhāri in
Al-'Adab Al-Mufrad, An-Nasā'i in *'Amalul-Yawm
wal-Laylah* and Ibn As-Sunni. Nasā'i's and Abu
Dawud's chains of transmission are good (*Hasan*),
Ibn Bāz, p.23.

٨١-«اللَّهُمَّ مَا أَصْبَحَ بِي مِنْ نِعْمَةٍ أَوْ بِأَحَدٍ مِنْ خَلْقِكَ فَمِنْكَ وَحْدَكَ لَا شَرِيكَ لَكَ، فَلَكَ الْحَمْدُ وَلَكَ الشُّكْرُ».

Allaahumma maa 'asbaha bee min ni'matin 'aw bi'ahadin min khalqika faminka wah-daka laa shareeka laka, falakal-hamdu wa lakash-shukru.

O Allāh, whatever blessing has been received by me or anyone of Your creation[108] is from You alone, You have no partner. All praise is for you and thanks is to You.[109]

◆

---

108. When you say this in the evening, you should say: *Allaahumma maa 'amsaa bee...*: "O Allāh, as I... enter this evening..."

109. Whoever recites this in the morning, has completed his obligation to thank Allāh for that day; and whoever says it in the evening, has completed his obligation for that night. Abu Dawud 4/318, An-Nasā'i *'Amal-ul-Yawm wal Laylah* (no. 7), Ibn As-Sunni (no. 41), Ibn Hibban (no. 2361). Its chain of transmission is good (*Hasan*), Ibn Bāz, p. 24.

٨٢-«اللَّهُمَّ عَافِنِي فِي بَدَنِي، اللَّهُمَّ عَافِنِي فِي سَمْعِي، اللَّهُمَّ عَافِنِي فِي بَصَرِي، لَا إِلَهَ إِلَّا أَنْتَ. اللَّهُمَّ إِنِّي أَعُوذُ بِكَ مِنَ الكُفْرِ والفَقْرِ وأَعُوذُ بِكَ مِنْ عَذَابِ الْقَبْرِ، لَا إِلَهَ إِلَّا أَنْتَ.»

Allaahumma 'aafinee fee badanee, Allaahumma 'aafinee fee sam'ee, Allaahumma 'aafinee fee basaree, laa 'ilaaha 'illaa 'Anta. Allaahumma 'innee 'a'oothu bika minal-kufri, walfaqri, wa 'a'oothu bika min 'athaabil-qabri, laa 'ilaaha 'illaa 'Anta.

O Allāh, make me healthy in my body. O Allāh, preserve for me my hearing. O Allāh, preserve for me my sight. There is none worthy of worship but You. O Allāh, I seek refuge in You from disbelief and poverty and I seek refuge in You from the punishment of the grave. There is none worthy of worship but You. (Recite three times in Arabic.)[110]

---

110. Abu Dawud 4/324, Aḥmad 5/42, An-Nasā'i, *'Amal-ul-Yawm wal-Laylah* (no. 22), Ibn As Sunni (no. 69), Al-Bukhāri *Al-'Adab Al-Mufrad*. Its chain of transmission is good (*Hasan*), Ibn Bāz, p. 26.

٨٣- ﴿حَسْبِـيَ اللّٰهُ لَا إِلٰهَ إِلَّا هُوَ عَلَيْهِ تَوَكَّلْتُ وَهُوَ رَبُّ الْعَرْشِ الْعَظِيمِ﴾

Hasbiyallaahu laa 'ilaaha 'illaa Huwa 'alayhi tawakkaltu wa Huwa Rabbul-'Arshil-'Adheem.

Allāh is sufficient for me. There is none worthy of worship but Him. I have placed my trust in Him, He is Lord of the Majestic Throne. (Recite seven times in Arabic.)[111]

---◆---

٨٤- «اللّٰهُمَّ إِنِّي أَسْأَلُكَ الْعَفْوَ وَالْعَافِيَةَ فِي الدُّنْيَا وَالْآخِرَةِ، اللّٰهُمَّ إِنِّي أَسْأَلُكَ الْعَفْوَ وَالْعَافِيَةَ فِي دِينِي وَدُنْيَايَ وَأَهْلِي، وَمَالِي، اللّٰهُمَّ اسْتُرْ عَوْرَاتِي، وَآمِنْ رَوْعَاتِي، اللّٰهُمَّ احْفَظْنِي مِنْ بَيْنِ يَدَيَّ، وَمِنْ خَلْفِي، وَعَنْ يَمِينِي، وَعَنْ شِمَالِي، وَمِنْ فَوْقِي، وَأَعُوذُ بِعَظَمَتِكَ أَنْ أُغْتَالَ مِنْ تَحْتِي».

---

111. Allāh will grant whoever recites this seven times in the morning or evening whatever he desires from this world or the next, Ibn As-Sunni (no. 71), Abu Dawud 4/321. Both reports are attributed directly to the Prophet ﷺ (Marfu'). The chain of transmission is sound (*Sahīh*). Ibn As-Sunni.

*Allaahumma 'innee 'as'alukal-'afwa wal'aafi-
yata fid-dunyaa wal'aakhirati, Allaahumma
'innee 'as'alukal-'afwa wal'aafiyata fee deenee
wa dunyaaya wa 'ah ee, wa maalee, Allaa-
hum-mastur 'awraatee, wa 'aamin raw'aatee,
Allaahummahfadhnee min bayni yadayya,
wa min khalfee, wa 'an yameenee, wa 'an
shimaalee, wa min fawqee, wa 'a'oothu
bi'adhamatika 'an 'ughtaala min tahtee.*

O Allāh, I seek Your forgiveness and Your
protection in this world and the next. O Allāh,
I seek Your forgiveness and Your protection
in my religion, in my worldly affairs, in my
family and in my wealth. O Allāh, conceal my
secrets and preserve me from anguish.
O Allāh, guard me from what is in front of
me and behind me, from my left, and from
my right, and from above me. I seek refuge in
Your Greatness from being struck down from
beneath me.[112]

---

112. *Sahīh Ibn Mājah* 2/332 and Abu Dawud.

٨٥-«اللَّهُمَّ عَالِمَ الْغَيْبِ وَالشَّهَادَةِ فَاطِرَ السَّمَوَاتِ
وَالأَرْضِ، رَبَّ كُلِّ شَيْءٍ وَمَلِيكَهُ، أَشْهَدُ أَنْ لَا إِلَهَ إِلَّا
أَنْتَ، أَعُوذُ بِكَ مِنْ شَرِّ نَفْسِي، وَمِنْ شَرِّ الشَّيْطَانِ وَشِرْكِهِ،
وَأَنْ أَقْتَرِفَ عَلَى نَفْسِي سُوءًا، أَوْ أَجُرَّهُ إِلَى مُسْلِمٍ».

*Allaahumma 'Aalimal-ghaybi wash shahaadati
faatiras-samaawaati wal'ardhi, Rabba kulli
shay'in wa maleekahu, 'ash hadu 'an laa 'ilaaha 'illaa 'Anta, 'a'oothu bika min sharri nafsee,
wa min sharrish-shaytaani wa shirkihi, wa 'an
'aqtarifa 'alaa nafsee soo'an, 'aw 'ajurrahu 'ilaa
Muslimin.*

O Allāh, Knower of the unseen and the evident,
Maker of the heavens and the earth, Lord of
everything and its Possessor, I bear witness
that there is none worthy of worship but You.
I seek refuge in You from the evil of my soul
and from the evil of Satan and his helpers.
(I seek refuge in You) from bringing evil upon
my soul and from harming any Muslim.[113]

---

113. *Sahīh At-Tirmithi* 3/142 and Abu Dawud.

٨٦-«بِسْمِ اللهِ الَّذِي لَا يَضُرُّ مَعَ اسْمِهِ شَيْءٌ فِي الْأَرْضِ
وَلَا فِي السَّمَاءِ وَهُوَ السَّمِيعُ الْعَلِيمُ».

*Bismillaahil-lathee laa yadhurru ma'asmihi
shay'un fil-'ardhi wa laa fis-samaa'i wa Hu-
was-Samee'ul-'Aleem.*

In the Name of Allāh, Who with His Name
nothing can cause harm in the earth nor in
the heavens, and He is the All-Hearing, the
All-Knowing. (Recite three times in Arabic.)[114]

◆

٨٧-«رَضِيتُ بِاللهِ رَبًّا، وَبِالْإِسْلَامِ دِينًا، وَبِمُحَمَّدٍ ﷺ نَبِيًّا».

*Radheetu billaahi Rabban, wa bil 'Islaami
deenan, wa bi-Muhammadin (sallallaahu
'alayhi wa sallama) Nabiyyan.*

---

114. "Whoever recites it three times in the morning will
    not be afflicted by any calamity before evening, and
    whoever recites it three times in the evening will not
    be overtaken by any calamity before morning." Abu
    Dawud 4/323, At-Tirmithi 5/465, Ibn Mājah 2/332,
    Aḥmad. Ibn Mājah's chain of transmission is good
    (*Hasan*), Ibn Bāz, p. 39.

I am pleased with Allāh as my Lord, with Islam as my religion and with Muhammad (peace and blessings of Allāh be upon him) as my Prophet. (Recite three times in Arabic.)[115]

•

٨٨-«يَا حَيُّ يَا قَيُّومُ بِرَحْمَتِكَ أَسْتَغِيثُ أَصْلِحْ لِي شَأْنِي كُلَّهُ وَلَا تَكِلْنِي إِلَى نَفْسِي طَرْفَةَ عَيْنٍ».

Yaa Hayyu yaa Qayyoomu birahmatika 'astagheethu 'aslih lee sha'nee kullahu wa laa takilnee 'ilaa nafsee tarfata 'aynin.

O Ever Living One, O Eternal One, by Your mercy I call on You to set right all my affairs. Do not place me in charge of my soul even for the blinking of an eye (i.e. a moment).[116]

---

115. "Allāh has promised that anyone who says this three times every morning or evening will be pleased on the Day of Resurrection." Aḥmad 4/337, An-Nasā'i, *'Amalul-Yawm wal-Laylah* p. 4, Ibn As-Sunni (no. 68), At-Tirmithi 5/465. Its chain of transmission is good (*Hasan*), Ibn Bāz, p. 39.

116. Its chain of transmission is sound (*Saḥīḥ*), Al-Ḥākim 1/545, see Albāni, *Saḥīhut-Targhib wat-Tarhib*, 1/273.

٨٩-«أَصْبَحْنَا وَأَصْبَحَ الْمُلْكُ للهِ رَبِّ الْعَالَمِينَ، اللَّهُمَّ إِنِّي
أَسْأَلُكَ خَيْرَ هَذَا الْيَوْمِ: فَتْحَهُ، وَنَصْرَهُ وَنُورَهُ، وَبَرَكَتَهُ،
وَهُدَاهُ، وَأَعُوذُ بِكَ مِنْ شَرِّ مَا فِيهِ وَشَرِّ مَا بَعْدَهُ».

*'Asbahnaa wa 'asbahal-mulku lillaahi Rab-
bil-'aalameen, Allaahumma 'innee 'as'aluka
khayra haathal-yawmi: Fathahu wa nasrahu
wa noorahu, wa barakatahu, wa hudaahu,
wa'a'oothu bika min sharri maa feehi wa
sharri maa ba'dahu.*

We have entered a new day and with it all the
dominion which belongs to Allāh, Lord of all
that exists. O Allāh, I ask You for the goodness of this day,[117] its victory, its help, its light,
its blessings, and its guidance. I seek refuge in
You from the evil that is in it and from the evil
that follows it.[118]

❖

---

117. For evening recitation, say here: *Allaahumma 'innee
'as'aluka khayra haathihil-laylati:* "My Lord, I ask
You for the good things of this night."

118. Abu Dawud 4/322. Its transmission chain is good
(*Hasan*). See also Ibn Al-Qayyim, *Zādul-Ma'ād* 2/273.

٩٠- «أَصْبَحْنَا عَلَى فِطْرَةِ الإِسْلَامِ وَعَلَى كَلِمَةِ الإِخْلَاصِ، وَعَلَى دِينِ نَبِيِّنَا مُحَمَّدٍ ﷺ، وَعَلَى مِلَّةِ أَبِينَا إِبْرَاهِيمَ، حَنِيفًا مُسْلِمًا وَمَا كَانَ مِنَ الْمُشْرِكِينَ».

'Asbahnaa 'alaa fitratil-'Islaami wa 'alaa kali-matil-'ikhlaasi, wa 'alaa deeni Nabiyyinaa Muhammadin (sallallaahu 'alayhi wa sallama), wa 'alaa millati 'abeenaa 'Ibraaheema, hanee-fan Musliman wa maa kaana minal-mushrikeen.

We have entered a new day[119] upon the natural religion of Islam, the word of sincere devotion, the religion of our Prophet Muhammad (peace and blessings of Allāh be upon him), and the faith of our father Ibrahim. He was upright (in worshipping Allāh), and a Muslim. He was not of those who worship others besides Allāh.[120]

--------------◆--------------

119. When you say this in the evening, you should say:
    'Amsaynaa 'alaafitratil-'Islaam... : "We end this day..."
120. Say: Amsaynaa 'alaafitratil-'Islaam... : "We end this day..."

٩١-«سُبْحَانَ اللهِ وَبِحَمْدِهِ».

Subhaanallaahi wa bihamdihi.

Glory is to Allāh and praise is to Him. (Recite one hundred times in Arabic.)[121]

••••••••••••••• • •••••••••••••••

٩٢-«لَا إِلَهَ إِلَّا اللهُ وَحْدَهُ لَا شَرِيكَ لَهُ، لَهُ الْمُلْكُ وَلَهُ الْحَمْدُ وَهُوَ عَلَى كُلِّ شَيْءٍ قَدِيرٌ».

Laa 'ilaaha 'illallaahu wahdahu laa shareeka lahu, lahul-mulku wa lahul-hamdu, wa Huwa 'alaa kulli shay'in Qadeer.

None has the right to be worshipped but Allāh alone, Who has no partner. His is the dominion and His is the praise and He is Able to do

121. "Whoever recites this one hundred times in the morning and in the evening will not be surpassed on the Day of Resurrection by anyone having done better than this except for someone who had recited it more." Al-Bukhāri 4/2071.

all things. (Recite ten times[122] in Arabic or one
time to ward off laziness.)[123]

---

122. Allāh will write ten *Hasanaat* (rewards) for whoever
recites this ten times in the morning, and forgive him
ten misdeeds and give him the reward of freeing ten
slaves and protect him from Satan. Whoever recites
this ten times in the evening will get this same reward.
An-Nasā'i, 'Amalul-Yawm wal-Laylah (no. 24). Its
chain of transmission is sound (*Sahīh*). Albāni 1/272.
Abu Hurayrah 🙵 narrated that the Prophet 🙵 said:
"Allāh will write one hundred *Hasanat* for whoever
says 'There is no god but Allāh alone; He has no
partner. To Allāh is possession of everything, and to
Him all praise is. He is Capable of all things' ten times
in the morning, and forgive him one hundred misdeeds.
He will have the reward of freeing a slave and will be
protected from Satan throughout the day unto dusk.
Whoever says it in the evening will have the same
reward." Aḥmad 8/704, 16/ 293. Its chain of transmission is good (*Hasan*), Ibn Bāz, p. 44.

123. Whoever recites this in the morning, will have the
reward of freeing a slave from the Children of Isma'il.
Ten *Hasanaat* (rewards) will be written fo him, and
he will be forgiven ten misdeeds, raised up ten degrees,
and be protected from Satan until evening. Whoever
says it in the evening will have the same reward until
morning. Abu Dawud 4/319, 3/957, Aḥmad 4/60,
Ibn Mājah 2/331, Ibn Al-Qayyim *Zādul- Ma'ād* 2/388.
Its chain of transmission is sound (*Sahīh*). Al-Albāni
1/270.

٩٣-«لَا إِلَهَ إِلَّا اللهُ وَحْدَهُ لَا شَرِيكَ لَهُ، لَهُ الْمُلْكُ وَلَهُ الْحَمْدُ وَهُوَ عَلَى كُلِّ شَيْءٍ قَدِيرٌ».

Laa 'ilaaha 'illallaahu wahdahu laa shareeka lahu, lahul-mulku wa lahul-hamdu wa Huwa 'alaa kulli shay'in Qadeer.

None has the right to be worshipped but Allāh alone, Who has no partner. His is the dominion and His is the praise and He is Able to do all things. (Recite one hundred times in Arabic upon rising in the morning.)[124]

- - - - - - - - - ♦ - - - - - - - -

٩٤-«سُبْحَانَ اللهِ وَبِحَمْدِهِ: عَدَدَ خَلْقِهِ، وَرِضَا نَفْسِهِ، وَزِنَةَ عَرْشِهِ وَمِدَادَ كَلِمَاتِهِ».

---

124. Whoever recites this one hundred times a day will have the reward of freeing ten slaves. One hundred *Hasanaat* (rewards) will be written for him and one hundred misdeeds will be washed away. He will be shielded from Satan until the evening. No one will be able to present anything better than this except for someone who has recited more than this. Al-Bukhāri 4/95, Muslim 4/2071.

SubhaanaUaahi wa bihamdihi: 'Adada khalqihi, wa ridhaa nafsihi, wa zinata 'arshihi wa midaa-da kalimaatihi.

Glory is to Allāh and praise is to Him, by the multitude of His creation, by His Pleasure, by the weight of His Throne, and by the extent of His Words. (Recite three times in Arabic upon rising in the morning.)[125]

◆

٩٥-«اللَّهُمَّ إِنِّي أَسْأَلُكَ عِلْمًا نَافِعًا ، وَرِزْقًا طَيِّبًا ، وَعَمَلًا مُتَقَبَّلًا» .

Allaahumma 'innee 'as'aluka 'ilman naafi'an, wa rizqan tayyiban, wa 'amalan mutaqabbalan.

O Allāh, I ask You for knowledge that is of benefit, a good provision, and deeds that will be accepted. (Recite in Arabic upon rising in the morning.)[126]

---

125. Muslim 4/2090.
126. Ibn As-Sunni, no. 54, Ibn Mājah no. 925. Its chain of transmission is good (*Hasan*), Ibn Al Qayyim 2/375.

٩٦-«أَسْتَغْفِرُ اللهَ وَأَتُوبُ إِلَيْهِ».

'Astaghfirullaaha wa 'atoobu 'ilayhi.

I seek the forgiveness of Allāh and repent to Him. (Recite one hundred times in Arabic during the day.)[127]

•

٩٧-«أَعُوذُ بِكَلِمَاتِ اللهِ التَّامَّاتِ مِنْ شَرِّ مَا خَلَقَ».

'A 'oothu bikalimaatil-laahit-taammaati min sharri maa khalaqa.

I seek refuge in the Perfect Words of Allāh from the evil of what He has created. (Recite three times in Arabic in the evening.)[128]

127. Al-Bukhāri, cf. Al-Asqalāni, *Fathul-Bāri* 11/101, Muslim 4/2075.

128. Whoever recites this three times in the evening will be protected from insect stings, Aḥmad 2/290, An-Nasā'i, *'Amalul-Yawm wal-Laylah* no. 590, At-Tirmithi 3/187, Ibn As-Sunni no. 68. According to Al-Albāni, Ibn Mājah's (2/266) chain of transmission is sound (*Ṣaḥīḥ*), and following Ibn Bāz 45, At-Tirmithi's report is good (*Hasan*).

٩٨-«اللّٰهُمَّ صَلِّ وَسَلِّمْ عَلَى نَبِيِّنَا مُحَمَّدٍ».

Allaahumma salli wa sallim 'alaa Nabiyyinaa Muhammadin.

O Allāh, we ask for your peace and blessings upon our Prophet Muhammad. (Recite ten times in Arabic.)[130]

---

130. The Prophet ﷺ said: "Who recites blessings upon me ten times in the morning and ten times in the evening will obtain my intercession on the Day of Resurrection." At-Tabarāni reported this *Hadith* together with two chains of transmission. One of them is reliable (*Jayyid*). See Haythami's *Majma 'uz-Zawā'id* 10/120, and Al-Albāni's *Sahīhut-Targhib wat-Tarhib* 1/273.

28. Before sleeping

(Cup your palms together, blow gently into them and then recite:)

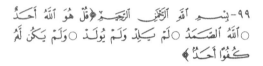

Bismillaahir-Rahmaanir-Raheem.
Qul Huwallaahu 'Ahad. Allaahus-Samad.
Lam yalid wa lam yoolad. Wa lam yakun lahu
kufuwan 'ahad.

With the Name of Allāh, the Most Gracious, the Most Merciful. Say: He is Allāh (the) One. The Self-Sufficient Master, Whom all creatures need, He begets not nor was He begotten, and none is equal to Him.

◆

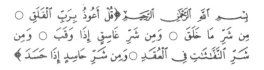

Bismillaahir-Rahmaanir-Raheem.
Qul 'a'oothu birabbil-falaq. Min sharri maa khalaq. Wa min sharri ghaasiqin 'ithaa waqab. Wa min sharrin-naffaathaati fil 'uqad. Wa min sharri haasidin 'ithaa hasad.

With the Name of Allāh, the Most Gracious, the Most Merciful. Say: I seek refuge with (Allāh) the Lord of the daybreak, from the evil of what He has created, and from the evil of the darkening (night) as it comes with its darkness, and from the evil of those who practice witchcraft when they blow in the knots, and from the evil of the envier when he envies.

بِسْمِ ٱللَّهِ ٱلرَّحْمَـٰنِ ٱلرَّحِيمِ ﴿قُلْ أَعُوذُ بِرَبِّ ٱلنَّاسِ ۝ مَلِكِ ٱلنَّاسِ ۝ إِلَـٰهِ ٱلنَّاسِ ۝ مِن شَرِّ ٱلْوَسْوَاسِ ٱلْخَنَّاسِ ۝ ٱلَّذِى يُوَسْوِسُ فِى صُدُورِ ٱلنَّاسِ ۝ مِنَ ٱلْجِنَّةِ وَٱلنَّاسِ﴾

Bismillaahir-Rahmaanir-Raheem.
Qul 'a'oothu birabbin-naas. Malikin-naas.
'Ilaahin-naas. Min sharril-waswaasil khan-
naas. Allathee yuwaswisu fee sudoorin-naas.
Minal-jinnati wannaas.

With the Name of Allāh, the Most Gracious,
the Most Merciful. Say: I seek refuge with
(Allāh) the Lord of mankind, the King of mankind, the God of mankind, from the evil of the
whisperer who withdraws, who whispers in the
breasts of mankind, of jinns and men.
(Then pass your hands over as much of your
body as you can reach, beginning with the head
and the face, then the entire front of your body.
Do this three times.)[131]

---

131. Al-Bukhāri, cf. Al-Asqalāni, *Fathul-Bāri* 9/62, and
Muslim 4/1723.

١٠٠- ﴿ٱللَّهُ لَآ إِلَٰهَ إِلَّا هُوَ ٱلۡحَىُّ ٱلۡقَيُّومُ لَا تَأۡخُذُهُۥ سِنَةٌ وَلَا نَوۡمٌ لَّهُۥ مَا فِى ٱلسَّمَٰوَٰتِ وَمَا فِى ٱلۡأَرۡضِ مَن ذَا ٱلَّذِى يَشۡفَعُ عِندَهُۥٓ إِلَّا بِإِذۡنِهِۦ يَعۡلَمُ مَا بَيۡنَ أَيۡدِيهِمۡ وَمَا خَلۡفَهُمۡ وَلَا يُحِيطُونَ بِشَىۡءٖ مِّنۡ عِلۡمِهِۦٓ إِلَّا بِمَا شَآءَ وَسِعَ كُرۡسِيُّهُ ٱلسَّمَٰوَٰتِ وَٱلۡأَرۡضَ وَلَا يَـُٔودُهُۥ حِفۡظُهُمَا وَهُوَ ٱلۡعَلِىُّ ٱلۡعَظِيمُ ﴾

Allaahu laa 'ilaaha 'illaa Huwal Hayyul-Qayyoom, laa ta'khuthuhu sinatun wa laa nawm, lahu maa fis-samaawaati wa maa fil-'ardh, man thal-lathee yashfa'u 'indahu 'illaa bi'ithnihi, ya'lamu maa bayna 'aydee-him wa maa khalfahum, wa laa yuheetoona bishay'im-min 'ilmihi 'illaa bimaa shaa'a, wasi'a kursiyyuhus-samaawaati wal'ardha, wa laa ya'ooduhu hifdhuhumaa, wa Huwal-'Ali-yyul-'Adheem.

Allāh! There is no god but He, the Ever Living, the One Who sustains and protects all that exists. Neither slumber nor sleep overtakes Him. To Him belongs whatever is in the heavens and whatever is on the earth. Who is he that can intercede with Him except with

His Permission? He knows what happens to them in this world, and what will happen to them in the Hereafter. And they will never encompass anything of His Knowledge except that which He wills. His Throne extends over the heavens and the earth, and He feels no fatigue in guarding and preserving them. And He is the Most High, the Most Great.[132]

---•---

١٠١ – ﴿ءَامَنَ ٱلرَّسُولُ بِمَآ أُنزِلَ إِلَيْهِ مِن رَّبِّهِ وَٱلْمُؤْمِنُونَ كُلٌّ ءَامَنَ بِٱللَّهِ وَمَلَـٰٓئِكَتِهِۦ وَكُتُبِهِۦ وَرُسُلِهِۦ لَا نُفَرِّقُ بَيْنَ أَحَدٍ مِّن رُّسُلِهِۦ وَقَالُوا۟ سَمِعْنَا وَأَطَعْنَا غُفْرَانَكَ رَبَّنَا وَإِلَيْكَ ٱلْمَصِيرُ ۞ لَا يُكَلِّفُ ٱللَّهُ نَفْسًا إِلَّا وُسْعَهَا لَهَا مَا كَسَبَتْ وَعَلَيْهَا مَا ٱكْتَسَبَتْ رَبَّنَا لَا تُؤَاخِذْنَآ إِن نَّسِينَآ أَوْ أَخْطَأْنَا رَبَّنَا وَلَا تَحْمِلْ عَلَيْنَآ إِصْرًا كَمَا حَمَلْتَهُۥ عَلَى ٱلَّذِينَ مِن قَبْلِنَا رَبَّنَا وَلَا تُحَمِّلْنَا مَا لَا طَاقَةَ لَنَا بِهِۦ وَٱعْفُ عَنَّا وَٱغْفِرْ لَنَا وَٱرْحَمْنَآ أَنتَ مَوْلَىٰنَا فَٱنصُرْنَا عَلَى ٱلْقَوْمِ ٱلْكَـٰفِرِينَ﴾

---

132. Al-Baqarah 2:255. Whoever reads this when he lies down to sleep will have a guardian from Allāh remain with him, and Satan will not be able to come near him until he rises in the morning.
See Al-Bukhāri, cf. Al-Asqalāni, *Fathul-Bāri* 4/487.

*'Aamanar-Rasoolu bimaa 'unzila 'ilayhi
mir- Rabbihi walmu'minoon, kullun 'aamana
billaahi wa malaa'ikatihi wa Kutubihi wa
Rusulihi, laa nufarriqu bayna 'ahadim-mir
Rusulihi, wa qaaloo sami'naa wa 'ata'naa
ghufraanaka Rabbanaa wa 'ilaykal-maseer.
Laa yukallifullaahu nafsan 'illaa wus'ahaa,
lahaa maa kasabat wa 'alayhaa mak tasabat,
Rabbanaa laa tu'aakhithnaa 'in naseenaa 'aw
'akhta'naa, Rabbanaa wa laa tahmil 'alaynaa
'isran kamaa hamaltahu 'alal-latheena min
qablinaa, Rabbanaa wa laa tuhammilnaa maa
laa taaqata lanaa bihi, wa'fu 'annaa, waghfir
lanaa warhamnaa, 'Anta Mawlaanaa fansur-
naa 'alal-qawmil kaafireen.*

The Messenger believes in what has been sent
down to him from his Lord, and so do the believers. Each one believes in Allāh, His Angels,
His Books, and His Messengers. They say:
"We make no distinction between any of His
Messengers," and they say: "We hear, and we
obey. (We seek) Your Forgiveness, our Lord,
and to You is the return." Allāh burdens

not a person beyond what he can bear. He gets reward for that (good) which he has earned, and he is punished for that (evil) which he has earned. Our Lord! Punish us not if we forget or fall into error. Our Lord! Lay not on us a burden like that which You did lay on those before us. Our Lord! Put not on us a burden greater than we have strength to bear. Pardon us and grant us forgiveness. Have mercy on us. You are our Protector, and help us against the disbelieving people.[133]

✦

١٠٢- «بِاسْمِكَ رَبِّي وَضَعْتُ جَنْبِي، وَبِكَ أَرْفَعُهُ، فَإِنْ أَمْسَكْتَ نَفْسِي فَارْحَمْهَا، وَإِنْ أَرْسَلْتَهَا فَاحْفَظْهَا، بِمَا تَحْفَظُ بِهِ عِبَادَكَ الصَّالِحِينَ».

Bismika Rabbee wadha'tu janbee, wa bika 'arfa'uhu, fa'in 'amsakta nafsee farhamhaa,

---

133. Al-Baqarah 2:285-6. These two verses will be sufficient for anyone who recites them at night before sleeping. Al-Bukhāri, cf. Al-Asqalāni, *Fathul-Bāri* 9/94, Muslim 1/554.

wa 'in 'arsaltahaa fahfadhhaa, bimaa tahfad-hu bihi 'ibaadakas-saaliheen.

With Your Name[134] my Lord, I lay myself down; and with Your Name I rise. And if my soul You take, have mercy on it, and if You send it back then protect it as You protect Your righteous slaves.[135]

◆

١٠٣-"اللَّهُمَّ إِنَّكَ خَلَقْتَ نَفْسِي وَأَنْتَ تَوَفَّاهَا، لَكَ مَمَاتُهَا وَمَحْيَاهَا، إِنْ أَحْيَيْتَهَا فَاحْفَظْهَا، وَإِنْ أَمَتَّهَا فَاغْفِرْ لَهَا. اللَّهُمَّ إِنِّي أَسْأَلُكَ الْعَافِيَةَ".

Allaahumma 'innaka khalaqta nafsee wa 'Anta tawaffaahaa, laka mamaatuhaa wa mahyaahaa, 'in 'ahyaytahaa fahfadhhaa, wa 'in 'amattahaa faghfir lahaa. Allaahumma 'innee 'as'alukal-'aafiyata.

134. "If any of you rises from his bed and later returns to it, let him dust off his bed with his waist garment three times and mention the Name of Allāh, for he does not know what may have entered the bed after him, and when he lies down he should say...".

135. Al-Bukhāri 11/126 and Muskim 4/2084.

O Allāh, You have created my soul and You take it back. Unto You is its death and its life. If You give it life then protect it, and if You cause it to die then forgive it. O Allāh, I ask You for strength.[136]

- - - - - - - - - ◆ - - - - - - - - -

١٠٤ - «اللَّهُمَّ قِنِي عَذَابَكَ يَوْمَ تَبْعَثُ عِبَادَكَ».

Allaahumma qinee 'athaabaka yawma tab'athu 'ibaadaka.

O Allāh,[137] save me from Your punishment on the Day that You resurrect Your slaves. (Recite three times in Arabic).[138]

- - - - - - - - - ◆ - - - - - - - - -

---

136. Muslim 4/2083 and Aḥmad 2/79.

137. "When the Prophet ﷺ lay down to sleep, he would place his right hand under his cheek and say..."

138. Abu Dawud 4/311. See also Al-Albāni, *Saḥīḥ At--Tirmithi* 3/143.

١٠٥ –«بِاسْمِكِ اللَّهُمَّ أَمُوتُ وَأَحْيَا» .

Bismika Allaahumma 'amootu wa 'ahyaa.

In Your Name, O Allāh, I die and I live.[139]

◆

١٠٦ –«سُبْحَانَ اللهِ، وَالْحَمْدُ للهِ، وَاللهُ أَكْبَرُ» .

Subhaanallaahi, Walhamdu lillaahi, Wallaahu 'Akbar.

Glory is to Allāh; Praise is to Allāh (thirty-three times); Allāh is the Most Great (thirty-four times) – in Arabic.[140]

---

139. Here, dying and living are metaphors for sleep and wakefulness. This explains why the normal order of these words has been reversed in this *Hadith*. In other contexts the living is mentioned before dying. See Qur'ān Al-Baqarah 2:258, Aal-'Imran 3: 156, Al-A'raf 7:158 among many other examples, (translator). See also Al-Asqalāni, *Fathul Bāri* 11/ 113, Muslim 4/2083.

140. Al-Bukhāri, cf. Al-Asqalāni, *Fathul-Bāri* 7/71, Muslim 4/2091.

١٠٧ـ«اللَّهُمَّ رَبَّ السَّمْوَاتِ السَّبْعِ وَرَبَّ الْعَرْشِ الْعَظِيمِ، رَبَّنَا وَرَبَّ كُلِّ شَيْءٍ، فَالِقَ الْحَبِّ وَالنَّوَى، وَمُنْزِلَ التَّوْرَاةِ وَالْإِنْجِيلِ، وَالْفُرْقَانِ، أَعُوذُ بِكَ مِنْ شَرِّ كُلِّ شَيْءٍ أَنْتَ آخِذٌ بِنَاصِيَتِهِ. اللَّهُمَّ أَنْتَ الْأَوَّلُ فَلَيْسَ قَبْلَكَ شَيْءٌ، وَأَنْتَ الْآخِرُ فَلَيْسَ بَعْدَكَ شَيْءٌ، وَأَنْتَ الظَّاهِرُ فَلَيْسَ فَوْقَكَ شَيْءٌ، وَأَنْتَ الْبَاطِنُ فَلَيْسَ دُونَكَ شَيْءٌ، اقْضِ عَنَّا الدَّيْنَ وَأَغْنِنَا مِنَ الْفَقْرِ».

Allaahumma Rabbas-samaawaatis sab'i wa Rabbal-'Arshil-'Adheem, Rabbanaa wa Rabba kulli shay'in, faaliqal-habbi wan-nawaa, wa munzilat-Tawraati wal 'Injeeli, wal-Furqaani, 'a'oothu bika min sharri kulli shay'in 'Anta 'aakhithun binaasiyatihi. Allaahumma 'Antal-'Awwalu falaysa qablaka shay'un, wa 'Antal-'Aakhiru falaysa ba'daka shay'un, wa 'Antadh Dhaahiru falaysa fawqaka shay'un, wa 'Antal-Baatinu falaysa doonaka shay'un, iqdhi 'annad-day-na wa 'aghninaa minal-faqri.

O Allāh! Lord of the seven heavens and Lord of the Magnificent Throne. Our Lord and the Lord of everything. Splitter of the grain and the date-stone, Revealer of the Torah and the Injeel[141] and the Furqān (the Qur'ān), I seek refuge in You from the evil of everything that You shall seize by the forelock.[142] O Allāh You are the First and nothing has come before you, and You are the Last, and nothing may come after You. You are the Most High, nothing is above You and You are the Most Near and nothing is nearer than You. Remove our debts from us and enrich us against poverty.[143]

---------◆---------

---

141. The Scripture that was revealed to 'Īsa (Jesus).
142. See Qur'ān Al-'Alaq 96:15, where seizure by the forelock preceeds being cast into Hell. (Translator)
143. Muslim 4/2084.

١٠٨-«الْحَمْدُ لله الَّذِي أَطْعَمَنَا وَسَقَانَا، وَكَفَانَا، وَآوَانَا، فَكَمْ مِمَّنْ لَا كَافِيَ لَهُ وَلَا مُؤْوِيَ».

Alhamdu lillaahil-lathee 'at'amanaa wa saqaanaa, wa kafaanaa, wa 'aawaanaa, fakam mimman laa kaafiya lahu wa laa mu'wiya.

Praise is to Allāh Who has provided us with food and with drink, sufficed us and gave us an abode, for how many are there with no provision and with no home.[144]

١٠٩-«اللَّهُمَّ عَالِمَ الْغَيْبِ وَالشَّهَادَةِ فَاطِرَ السَّمٰوَاتِ وَالْأَرْضِ، رَبَّ كُلِّ شَيْءٍ وَمَلِيكَهُ، أَشْهَدُ أَنْ لَا إِلٰهَ إِلَّا أَنْتَ، أَعُوذُ بِكَ مِنْ شَرِّ نَفْسِي، وَمِنْ شَرِّ الشَّيْطَانِ وَشِرْكِهِ، وَأَنْ أَقْتَرِفَ عَلَى نَفْسِي سُوءًا، أَوْ أَجُرَّهُ إِلَى مُسْلِمٍ».

Allaahumma 'Aalimal-ghaybi wash shahaa-dati faatiras-samaawaati wal'ardhi,

---

144. Muslim 4/2085.

Rabba kulli shay'in wa maleekahu, 'ashhadu 'an laa 'ilaaha 'illaa 'Anta, 'a'oothu bika min sharri nafsee, wa min sharrish-shaytaani wa shirkihi, wa 'an 'aqtarifa 'alaa nafsee soo'an, 'aw 'ajurrahu 'ilaa Muslimin.

O Allāh, Knower of the unseen and the evident, Maker of the heavens and the earth, Lord of everything and its Master, I bear witness that there is none worthy of worship but You. I seek refuge in You from the evil of my soul and from the evil of Satan and his helpers. (I seek refuge in You) from bringing evil upon my soul and from harming any Muslim.[145]

Recite *Surah 32 –As-Sajdah* and *Surah 67 – Al-Mulk* in Arabic.[146]

---

145. Abu Dawud 4/317. See also Al-Albāni, *Sahīh At--Tirmithi* 3/142.

146. At-Tirmithi, An-Nasā'i. See also Al-Albāni *Sahīhul-Jāmi' As-Saghīr* 4/25.

١١١-«اللَّهُمَّ أَسْلَمْتُ نَفْسِي إِلَيْكَ، وَفَوَّضْتُ أَمْرِي إِلَيْكَ، وَوَجَّهْتُ وَجْهِي إِلَيْكَ، وَأَلْجَأْتُ ظَهْرِي إِلَيْكَ، رَغْبَةً وَرَهْبَةً إِلَيْكَ، لَا مَلْجَأَ وَلَا مَنْجَا مِنْكَ إِلَّا إِلَيْكَ، آمَنْتُ بِكِتَابِكَ الَّذِي أَنْزَلْتَ وَنَبِيِّكَ الَّذِي أَرْسَلْتَ».

*Allaahumma 'aslamtu nafse 'ilayka, wa faw-
wadhtu 'amree 'ilayka, wa wajjahtu wajhee 'ilayka, wa 'alja'tu dhahree 'ilayka, raghbatan wa
rahbatan 'ilayka, laa malja' wa laa manja minka 'illaa 'ilayka, 'aamantu bikitaabikal-lathee
'anzalta wa bi-nabiyyikal-lathee 'arsalta.*

O Allāh,[147] I submit myself to You, entrust
my affairs to You, turn my face to You, and
lay myself down depending upon You, hoping
in You and fearing You. There is no refuge
and no escape, except to You. I believe in
Your Book (the Qur'ān) that You revealed,
and the Prophet whom You sent.[148]

---

147. "Before you go to bed perform ablutions as you
would for prayer, then lie down on your right side
and say…"

148. The Prophet ﷺ said: "Whoever says this and dies in

29. If you stir in the night

١١٢-«لَا إِلَهَ إِلَّا اللهُ الْوَاحِدُ الْقَهَّارُ، رَبُّ السَّمٰوَاتِ وَالْأَرْضِ وَمَا بَيْنَهُمَا الْعَزِيزُ الْغَفَّارُ».

Laa 'ilaaha 'illallaahul-Waahidul Qahhaaru, Rabbus-samaawaati wal'ardhi wa maa bayna-humal-'Azeezul-Ghaffaaru.

There is none worthy of worship but Allāh, the One, the Victorious, Lord of the heavens and the earth and all that is between them, the All-Mighty, the All-Forgiving.[149]

◆

his sleep, has died in a state of the natural monothe-ism (*Fitrah*)." Al-Bukhāri, cf. Al Asqalāni, *Fathul-Bāri* 11/113, Muslim 4/2081.

149. This is to be said if you turn over in bed during the night. Al-Hākim graded it authentic and Ath-Thahabi agreed 1/540. Also see An-Nasā'i, *'Amalul-Yawm wal-Laylah*, and Ibn As-Sunni. See also Al-Albāni, *Sahihul-Jāmi' As-Saghir* 4/213.

30. When afraid to go to sleep or feel lonely and depressed

١١٣-«أَعُوذُ بِكَلِمَاتِ اللهِ التَّامَّاتِ مِنْ غَضَبِهِ وَعِقَابِهِ،
وَشَرِّ عِبَادِهِ، وَمِنْ هَمَزَاتِ الشَّيَاطِينِ وَأَنْ يَحْضُرُونِ».

’A‘oothu bikalimaatil-laahit-taammaati min ghadhabihi wa ‘iqaabihi, wa sharri ‘ibaadihi, wa min hamazaatish-shayaateeni wa ’an yahdhuroon.

I seek refuge in the Perfect Words of Allāh from His anger and His punishment, from the evil of His slaves and from the taunts of devils and from their presence.[150]

------------◆------------

---

150. Abu Dawud 4/12. See also Al-Albāni, *Sahīh At-Tirmithi* 3/171.

31. After a bad dream or nightmare

Spit to your left (three times).[151]
Seek refuge in Allāh from the Devil and from
the evil of what you have seen (three times).[152]
Do not speak about it to anyone.[153]
Turn over on your other side.[154]
Get up and pray if you desire to do so.[155]

------------------------◆------------------------

32. For *Qunut* in the Witr *Salat*

١١٦- «اللّهُمَّ اهْدِنِي فِيمَنْ هَدَيْتَ، وَعَافِنِي فِيمَنْ عَافَيْتَ،
وَتَوَلَّنِي فِيمَنْ تَوَلَّيْتَ، وَبَارِكْ لِي فِيمَا أَعْطَيْتَ، وَقِنِي شَرَّ
مَا قَضَيْتَ، فَإِنَّكَ تَقْضِي وَلَا يُقْضَى عَلَيْكَ، إِنَّهُ لَا يَذِلُّ
مَنْ وَالَيْتَ، [وَلَا يَعِزُّ مَنْ عَادَيْتَ]، تَبَارَكْتَ رَبَّنَا
وَتَعَالَيْتَ».

---

151. Muslim 4/1772.
152. Muslim 4/1772,3.
153. Muslim 4/1772.
154. Muslim 4/1773.
155. Muslim 4/1773.

*Allaahum-mahdinee feeman hadayta, wa
'aafinee feeman 'aafayta, wa tawallanee
feeman tawallayta, wa baarik lee feemaa
'a'atayta, wa qinee sharra maa qadhayta,
fa'innaka taqdhee wa laa yuqdhaa 'alayka,
'innahu laa yathillu man waalayta, [wa laa
ya'izzu man 'aadayta], tabaarakta Rabbanaa wa ta'aalayta.*

O Allāh, guide me with those whom You
have guided, and strengthen me with those
whom You have given strength. Take me to
Your care with those whom You have taken
to Your care. Bless me in what You have
given me. Protect me from the evil You have
ordained. Surely, You command and are
not commanded, and none whom You have
committed to Your care shall be humiliated
[and none whom You have taken as an en-
emy shall taste glory]. You are Blessed, Our
Lord, and Exalted.[156]

---

156. Abu Dawud, Ibn Mājah, An-Nasā'i, At-Tirmithi,
Aḥmad, Ad-Dārimi, Al-Ḥākim, and Al-Bayhaqi'.
See also Al-Albāni, *Ṣaḥīḥ At-Tirmithi* 1/144, *Ṣaḥīḥ
Ibn Mājah* 1/194, and *'Irwa'ul-Ghalīl* 2/172.

١١٧ -«اللّٰهُمَّ إِنِّي أَعُوذُ بِرِضَاكَ مِنْ سَخَطِكَ، وَبِمُعَافَاتِكَ مِنْ عُقُوبَتِكَ، وَأَعُوذُ بِكَ مِنْكَ، لَا أُحْصِي ثَنَاءً عَلَيْكَ، أَنْتَ كَمَا أَثْنَيْتَ عَلَى نَفْسِكَ».

Allaahumma 'innee 'a'oothu biridhaaka min sakhatika, wa bimu'aafaatika min 'uqoo-batika, wa 'a'oothu bika minka, laa 'uhsee thanaa'an 'alayka, 'Anta kamaa 'athnayta 'alaa nafsika.

O Allāh, I seek refuge with Your Pleasure from Your anger. I seek refuge in Your forgiveness from Your punishment. I seek refuge in You from You. I cannot count Your praises, You are as You have praised Yourself.[157]

---

157. Abu Dawud, Ibn Mājah, An-Nasā'i, At-Tirmithi, Aḥmad. See Al-Albāni, *Ṣaḥīḥ At-Tirmithi* 3/180, *Ṣaḥīḥ Ibn Mājah* 1/194, and *'Irwa'ul-Ghalīl* 2/175.

١١٨-«اللَّهُمَّ إِيَّاكَ نَعْبُدُ، وَلَكَ نُصَلِّي وَنَسْجُدُ، وَإِلَيْكَ نَسْعَى وَنَحْفِدُ، نَرْجُو رَحْمَتَكَ، وَنَخْشَى عَذَابَكَ، إِنَّ عَذَابَكَ بِالْكَافِرِينَ مُلْحَقٌ. اللَّهُمَّ إِنَّا نَسْتَعِينُكَ، وَنَسْتَغْفِرُكَ، وَنُثْنِي عَلَيْكَ الْخَيْرَ، وَلَا نَكْفُرُكَ، وَنُؤْمِنُ بِكَ، وَنَخْضَعُ لَكَ، وَنَخْلَعُ مَنْ يَكْفُرُكَ».

Allaahumma 'iyyaaka na'budu, wa laka nusallee wa nasjudu, wa'ilayka nas'aa wa nahfidu, narjoo rahmataka, wa nakhshaa 'athaabaka, 'inna 'athaabaka bilkaafireena mulhaq. Allaahumma 'innaa nasta'eenuka, wa nastaghfiruka, wa nuthnee 'alaykal-khayr, wa laa nakfuruka, wa nu'minu bika, wa nakhdha'u laka, wa nakhla'u man yakfuruka.

O Allāh, You alone do we worship and to You we pray and bow down prostrate. To You we hasten to worship and to serve. Our hope is for Your mercy and we fear Your punishment. Surely, Your punishment of the disbelievers is at hand. O Allāh, we seek Your help and Your forgiveness, and we praise You beneficently. We do not deny You and we believe in You. We surrender to You and renounce whoever disbelieves in You.[158]

———————— • ————————

33. After the *Witr Salat*

١١٩- «سُبْحَانَ الْمَلِكِ الْقُدُّوسِ».

Subhaanal-Malikil-Quddoosi.

Glory is to the King, the Holy.
[Recite three times in Arabic, and raise and extend the voice on the third time and say...]

«رَبِّ الْمَلَائِكَةِ وَالرُّوحِ».

Rabbil-malaa'ikati warroohi.

Lord of the angels and the Spirit.[159]

---

158. Al-Bayhaqi graded its chain authentic in *As Sunan Al-Kubrā*. Al-Albāni said in *'Irwa'ul-Ghalīl* 2/170 that its chain is authentic as a statement of 'Umar.

159. An-Nasā'i 3/244, Ad-Dāraqutni and others. The final addition is from Ad-Daraqutni's version 2/31 and its chain of narration is authentic. See the checking of *Zādul-Ma'ād* by Shu'aib Al-Ama'ut and 'Abdul-Qādir Al-Arna'ut 1/337.

34. In times of worry and grief

١٢٠- «اللَّهُمَّ إِنِّي عَبْدُكَ، ابْنُ عَبْدِكَ، ابْنُ أَمَتِكَ، نَاصِيَتِي بِيَدِكَ، مَاضٍ فِيَّ حُكْمُكَ، عَدْلٌ فِيَّ قَضَاؤُكَ، أَسْأَلُكَ بِكُلِّ اسْمٍ هُوَ لَكَ، سَمَّيْتَ بِهِ نَفْسَكَ، أَوْ أَنْزَلْتَهُ فِي كِتَابِكَ، أَوْ عَلَّمْتَهُ أَحَدًا مِنْ خَلْقِكَ، أَوِ اسْتَأْثَرْتَ بِهِ فِي عِلْمِ الْغَيْبِ عِنْدَكَ، أَنْ تَجْعَلَ الْقُرْآنَ رَبِيعَ قَلْبِي، وَنُورَ صَدْرِي، وَجَلَاءَ حُزْنِي، وَذَهَابَ هَمِّي».

Allaahumma 'innee 'abduka, ibnu 'abdika, ibnu 'amatika, naasiyatee biyadika, maadhin fiyya hukmuka, 'adlun fiyya qadhaa'uka, 'as'aluka bikulli ismin huwa laka, sammayta bihi nafsaka, 'aw 'anzaltahu fee kitaabika, 'aw 'allamtahu 'ahadan min khalqika, 'awista'thar-ta bihi fee 'ilmil-ghaybi 'indaka, 'an taj'alal-Qur'āna rabee'a qalbee, wa noora sadree, wa jalaa'a huznee, wa tha̲haaba hammee.

O Allāh, I am Your slave and the son of Your male slave and the son of your female slave. My forehead is in Your Hand (i.e. you have control over me). Your Judgment upon me is assured and Your Decree concerning me is just. I ask You by every Name that You have named Yourself with, revealed in Your Book, taught any one of Your creation or kept unto Yourself in the knowledge of the unseen that is with You, to make the Qur'ān the spring of my heart, and the light of my chest, the banisher of my sadness and the reliever of my distress.[160]

---•---

١٢١–«اللَّهُمَّ إِنِّي أَعُوذُ بِكَ مِنَ الْهَمِّ وَالْحَزَنِ، وَالْعَجْزِ وَالْكَسَلِ، وَالْبُخْلِ وَالْجُبْنِ، وَضَلَعِ الدَّيْنِ وَغَلَبَةِ الرِّجَالِ».

Allaahumma 'innee 'a'oothu bika minal hammi walhazani, wal'ajzi walkasali, walbukhli waljub-ni, wa dhala'id-dayni wa ghalabatir-rijaal.

O Allāh, I seek refuge in you from grief and sadness, from weakness and from laziness, from miserliness and from cowardice, from being overcome by debt and overpowered by men (i.e. others).[161]

---

160. Aḥmad 1/391, and Al-Albāni graded it authentic.
161. Al-Bukhāri 7/158. See also Al-Asqalāni, *Fathul-Bāri* 11/173.

35. When in anguish

١٢٢-«لَا إِلَهَ إِلَّا اللهُ الْعَظِيمُ الْحَلِيمُ، لَا إِلَهَ إِلَّا اللهُ رَبُّ الْعَرْشِ الْعَظِيمِ، لَا إِلَهَ إِلَّا اللهُ رَبُّ السَّمَوَاتِ وَرَبُّ الأَرْضِ وَرَبُّ الْعَرْشِ الْكَرِيمِ»

Laa 'ilaaha 'illallahul-'Adheemul Haleem, laa 'ilaaha 'illallaahu Rabbul-'Arshil 'Adheem, laa 'ilaaha 'illallaahu Rabbus samaawaati wa Rabbul-'ardhi wa Rabbul 'Arshil-Kareem.

There is none worthy of worship but Allāh the Mighty, the Forbearing. There is none worthy of worship but Allāh, Lord of the Magnificent Throne. There is none worthy of worship but Allāh, Lord of the heavens and Lord of the earth, and Lord of the Noble Throne.[162]

⬩

١٢٣-«اللَّهُمَّ رَحْمَتَكَ أَرْجُو فَلَا تَكِلْنِي إِلَى نَفْسِي طَرْفَةَ عَيْنٍ، وَأَصْلِحْ لِي شَأْنِي كُلَّهُ، لَا إِلَهَ إِلَّا أَنْتَ».

---

162. Al-Bukhāri 8/154, Muslim 4/2092.

*Allaahumma rahmataka 'arjoo falaa takilnee
'ilaa nafsee tarfata 'aynin, wa 'aslih lee sha'nee
kullahu, laa'ilaaha 'illaa 'Anta.*

O Allāh, I hope for Your mercy. Do not leave
me to myself even for the blinking of an eye (i.e.
a moment). Correct all of my affairs for me.
There is none worthy of worship but You.[163]

١٢٤-«لَا إِلَهَ إِلَّا أَنْتَ سُبْحَانَكَ إِنِّي كُنْتُ مِنَ الظَّالِمِينَ».

*Laa 'ilaaha 'illaa 'Anta subhaanaka 'innee
kuntu minadh-dhaalimeen.*

There is none worthy of worship but You,
glory is to You. Surely, I was among the
wrongdoers.[164]

---

163. Abu Dawud 4/324, Aḥmad 5/42. Al-Albāni graded it
     as good in *Sahīh Abu Dawud* 3/959.
164. At-Tirmithi 5/529. Al-Hākim declared it authentic
     and Ath-Thahabi agreed with him 1/505. See also
     Al-Albāni, *Sahīh At-Tirmithi* 3/168.

١٢٥ - «اللهُ اللهُ رَبِّي لَا أُشْرِكُ بِهِ شَيْئًا».

Allaahu Allaahu Rabbee laa 'ush riku bihi shay'an.

Allāh, Allāh is my Lord. I do not associate anything with Him.[165]

---

36. On meeting an adversary or a brutal ruler

١٢٦ - «اللَّهُمَّ إِنَّا نَجْعَلُكَ فِي نُحُورِهِمْ وَنَعُوذُ بِكَ مِنْ شُرُورِهِمْ».

Allaahumma 'innaa naj'aluka fee nuhoorihim wa na'oothu bika min shuroorihim.

O Allāh, we ask You to restrain them by their necks and we seek refuge in You from their evil.[166]

---

165. Abu Dawud 2/87. See also Al-Albāni, *Sahīh Ibn Mājah* 2/335.
166. Abu Dawud 2/89, and Al-Hākim graded it authentic and Ath-Thahabi agreed 2/142.

١٢٧ –«اللَّهُمَّ أَنْتَ عَضُدِي، وَأَنْتَ نَصِيرِي، بِكَ أَجُولُ،
وَبِكَ أَصُولُ، وَبِكَ أُقَاتِلُ».

Allaahumma 'Anta 'adhudee, wa 'Anta naseeree, bika 'ajoolu, wa bika 'asoolu, wa bika 'uqaatilu.

O Allāh, You are my strength and You are my support. For Your sake I go forth and for Your sake I advance and for Your sake I fight.[167]

◆

١٢٨ –«حَسْبُنَا اللهُ وَنِعْمَ الْوَكِيلُ».

Hasbunallāhu wa ni'amal-wakeel.

Allāh is sufficient for us and the best of those on whom to depend.[168]

---

167. Dawud 3/42, At-Tirmithi 5/572. See also Al-Albāni, *Sahīh At-Tirmithi* 3/183.

168. Al-Bukhāri, 5/172.

37. Against the oppressors

١٢٩-«اللَّهُمَّ رَبَّ السَّمَواتِ السَّبْعِ، وَرَبَّ الْعَرْشِ الْعَظِيمِ، كُنْ لِي جَارًا مِنْ فُلَانِ بْنِ فُلَانٍ، وَأَحْزَابِهِ مِنْ خَلَائِقِكَ؛ أَنْ يَفْرُطَ عَلَيَّ أَحَدٌ مِنْهُمْ أَوْ يَطْغَى، عَزَّ جَارُكَ، وَجَلَّ ثَنَاؤُكَ، وَلَا إِلَهَ إِلَّا أَنْتَ».

Allaahumma Rabbas-samaawaatis sab'i, wa Rabbal-'Arshil-'Adheem, kun lee jaaran min [mention the person's name], wa 'ahzaabihi min khalaa'iqika, 'an yafruta 'alayya 'ahadun minhum 'aw yatghaa, 'azza jaaruka, wa jalla thanaa'uka, wa laa 'ilaaha 'illaa 'Anta.

O Allāh, Lord of the seven heavens, Lord of the Magnificent Throne, be for me a support against [such and such a person] and his helpers from among your creatures, lest any of them abuse me or do me wrong. Mighty is Your patronage and glorious are Your praises. There is none worthy of worship but You.[169]

---

169. Al-Bukhāri, *Al-'Adab Al-Mufrad* (no. 707). Al-Albāni graded it authentic in *Sahīh Al-'Adab Al-Mufrad* (no. 545).

١٣٠-"اللهُ أَكْبَرُ، اللهُ أَعَزُّ مِنْ خَلْقِهِ جَمِيعًا، اللهُ أَعَزُّ مِمَّا
أَخَافُ وَأَحْذَرُ، أَعُوذُ بِاللهِ الَّذِي لَا إِلَهَ إِلَّا هُوَ، الْمُمْسِكِ
السَّمَوَاتِ السَّبْعَ أَنْ يَقَعْنَ عَلَى الْأَرْضِ إِلَّا بِإِذْنِهِ، مِنْ شَرِّ
عَبْدِكَ فُلَانٍ، وَجُنُودِهِ وَأَتْبَاعِهِ وَأَشْيَاعِهِ، مِنَ الْجِنِّ
وَالْإِنْسِ، اللَّهُمَّ كُنْ لِي جَارًا مِنْ شَرِّهِمْ، جَلَّ ثَنَاؤُكَ وَعَزَّ
جَارُكَ، وَتَبَارَكَ اسْمُكَ، وَلَا إِلَهَ غَيْرُكَ".

*Allaahu 'Akbar, Allāhu 'a'azzu min khalqihi
jamee'an, Allaahu 'a'azzu mimmaa 'akhaafu
wa 'ahtharu, 'a'oothu billaahil lathee laa
'ilaaha 'illaa Huwa, almumsikis- samaawaa-
tis-sab'i 'an yaqa'na 'alal-'ardhi 'illaa bi'ithnihi, min sharri 'abdika [name of the person],
wa junoodihi wa 'atbaa'ihi wa 'ashyaa'ihi,
minal-jinni wal'insi, Allaahumma kun lee
jaaran min sharrihim, jalla thanaa'uka wa
'azza jaaruka, wa tabaarakasmuka, wa laa
'ilaaha ghayruka.*

Allāh is the Most Great, Mightier than all
His creation. He is Mightier than what I fear
and dread. I seek refuge in Allāh, Who there
is none worthy of worship but Him. He is the

One Who holds the seven heavens from falling upon the earth except by His command. [I seek refuge in You Allāh] from the evil of Your slave [name of the person], and his helpers, his followers and his supporters from among the jinn and mankind. O Allāh, be my support against their evil. Glorious are Your praises and mighty is Your patronage. Blessed is Your Name, there is no true God but You. (Recite three times in Arabic.[170]

---

38. Against an enemy

١٣١-«اللَّهُمَّ مُنْزِلَ الْكِتَابِ، سَرِيعَ الْحِسَابِ، اهْزِمِ الْأَحْزَابَ، اللَّهُمَّ اهْزِمْهُمْ وَزَلْزِلْهُمْ».

Allaahumma munzilal-kitaabi, saree'al hisaabi, ihzimil-'ahzaaba, Allaahumma ihzimhum wa zalzilhum.

---

170. Al-Bukhāri, *Al-'Adab Al-Mufrad* (no. 708). Al-Albāni graded it authentic in *Sahīh Al-'Adab Al-Mufrad* (no. 546).

O Allāh, Revealer of the Book, Swift to account, defeat the groups (of enemies). O Allāh, defeat them and shake them.[171]

---

39. If you fear people may harm you

١٣٢- «اللّٰهُمَّ اكْفِنِيهِمْ بِمَا شِئْتَ».

Allaahummak-fineehim bimaa shi'ta.

O Allāh, suffice (i.e. protect) me against them however You wish.[172]

---

171. Muslim 3/1362.
172. Muslim 4/2300.

40. If stricken by in your faith

133. (Say:) I seek refuge in Allāh. (Then you should desist from doing what you are in doubt about).[173]

◆

١٣٤ -«آمَنْتُ بِاللهِ وَرُسُلِهِ».

'Aamantu billaahi wa Rusulihi.

(Say:) I believe in Allāh and His Messenger.[174]

◆

١٣٥ -﴿هُوَ ٱلْأَوَّلُ وَٱلْآخِرُ وَٱلظَّاهِرُ وَٱلْبَاطِنُ وَهُوَ بِكُلِّ شَيْءٍ عَلِيمٌ﴾

Huwal-'Awwalu wal-'Aakhiru wadh Dhaaa-hiru wal-Baatinu, wa Huwa bikulli shay'in 'Aleem.

(Recite the Ayat in Arabic).

---

173. Al-Bukhari, cf. Al-Asqalāni, *Fathul-Bāri* 6/336, Muslim 1/120.

174. Muslim, 1/119-20.

He is the First and the Last, the Most High and the Most Near. And He is the Knower of all things.[175]

---

41. For clearing the debt

١٣٦- «اللَّهُمَّ اكْفِنِي بِحَلَالِكَ عَنْ حَرَامِكَ وَأَغْنِنِي بِفَضْلِكَ عَمَّنْ سِوَاكَ».

Allaahummak-finee bihalaalika 'an haraamika wa 'aghninee bifadhlika 'amman siwaaka.

O Allāh, suffice me with what You have allowed instead of what You have forbidden, and make me independent of all others besides You.[176]

١٣٧- «اللَّهُمَّ إِنِّي أَعُوذُ بِكَ مِنَ الْهَمِّ وَالْحَزَنِ، وَالْعَجْزِ وَالْكَسَلِ، وَالْبُخْلِ وَالْجُبْنِ، وَضَلَعِ الدَّيْنِ وَغَلَبَةِ الرِّجَالِ».

---

175. Al-Hadid 57:3, Abu Dawud 4/329. Al-Albāni graded it good in *Sahīh Abu Dawud*, 3/962.
176. At-Tirmithi 5/560.
See also Al-Albāni, *Sahīh At-Tirmithi* 3/180.

Allaahumma 'innee 'a'oothu bika minal ham-mi walhazani, wal'ajzi walkasali, walbukhli waljubni, wa dhala'id-dayni wa ghalabatir-rijaali.

O Allāh, I seek refuge in You from grief and sadness, from weakness and from laziness, from miserliness and from cowardice, from being overcome by debt and from being over-powered by men (i.e. other people).[177]

---

42. When Satan distracts you during the Salat or Qur'ān recitation

١٣٨-«أَعُوذُ بِاللهِ مِنَ الشَّيْطَانِ الرَّجِيمِ».

'A'oothu billaahi minash-Shaytaanir-rajeem.

(Say:) I seek refuge in Allāh from Satan the outcast (then spit to your left). (Do this three times reciting in Arabic.[178]

---

177. Al-Bukhāri 7/158.
178. Muslim 4/1729.

43. When something gets difficult

١٣٩ -«اللَّهُمَّ لَا سَهْلَ إِلَّا مَا جَعَلْتَهُ سَهْلًا وَأَنْتَ تَجْعَلُ الْحَزْنَ إِذَا شِئْتَ سَهْلًا».

Allaahumma laa sahla 'illaa maa ja'altahu sahl-an wa 'Anta taj'alul-hazna 'ithaa shi'ta sahlan.

O Allāh, there is no ease other than what You make easy. If You please You ease sorrow.[179]

-------- ◆ --------

44. If you commit a sin

When a slave of Allāh commits a sin, but then prays two *Rak'ahs* and seeks Allāh's forgiveness with a firm resolution not to commit it again, Allāh will forgive him.[180]

---

179. Ibn Hibban in his *Sahīh* (no. 2427), and Ibn As Sunni (no. 351). Al-Hafidh (Ibn Hajar) said that this *Hadith* is authentic. It was also declared authentic by 'Abdul-Qadir Al-Arna'ut in his checking of An-Nawawi's *Kitābul-Athkār*, p. 106.

180. Abu Dawud 2/86, At-Tirmithi 2/257. Al-Albāni graded it authentic in *Sahīh Abu Dawud* 1/283.

45. Against Satan's promptings

Seek refuge with Allāh against Satan by saying:
I seek refuge in Allāh from Satan the outcast.[181]

The call to prayer – 'Athān.[182]

Saying words of Allāh's remembrance (Thikr)
and recitation of the Qur'ān.[183]

---

181. Abu Dawud 1/206, At-Tirmithi. See also Al-Albāni,
Sahīh At-Tirmithi 1/77, and *Surat Al-Mu'minūn*,
23:98-9.

182. Muslim 1/291, Al-Bukhāri 1/151.

183. "Do not turn your homes into graveyards, surely the
Devil flees from the house in which *Surat Al-Baqarah*
is read," Muslim 1/539. The Devil is also driven out
by the invocations for morning and evening, those
that are said before sleeping and upon waking up,
those for entering and leaving the house, including
those for entering and leaving the mosque, and by
many other authentic invocations taught to us by
the Prophet ﷺ such as the reading of 'Āyatul-Kursi,
(Al-Baqarah 2:255), and the last two 'Āyat of Surat
Al-Baqarah before going to sleep. Whoever says one
hundred times: "There is none worthy of worship
but Allāh alone, Who has no partner, His is the dominion and His is the praise, and he is Able to do all
things," it will be a protection for him from the Devil
throughout the day.

46. When something unfortunate happens, or when you fail to achieve something

١٤٤- «قَدَرُ اللهِ وَمَا شَاءَ فَعَلَ» .

Qadarullaahi wa maa shaa'a fa'ala.

It is the Decree of Allāh and He does whatever He wills.[184]

---------◆---------

---

184. "The strong believer is better and more dear to Allāh than the weak believer, and in each of them there is good. Be vigilant for what is to your benefit and seek the help of Allāh and do not falter. But when you are stricken by some setback, do not say: 'If only I had done such and such,' rather say: 'It is the Decree of Allāh and He does whatever He wills.' For verily the saying 'if (i.e. if only I had) begins the work of the Devil." Muslim 4/2052.

47. For congratulating new parents, and how they should respond

١٤٥-«بَارَكَ اللهُ لَكَ فِي الْمَوْهُوبِ لَكَ، وَشَكَرْتَ الْوَاهِبَ، وَبَلَغَ أَشُدَّهُ، وَرُزِقْتَ بِرَّهُ».

Baarakallaahu laka fil-mawhoobi laka, wa shakartal-waahiba, wa balagha 'ashuddahu, wa ruziqta birrahu.

May Allāh bless you with His gift to you, and may you (the new parent) give thanks, may the child reach the maturity of years, and may you be granted its righteousness.

The reply of the person being congratulated is to say:

«بَارَكَ اللهُ لَكَ وَبَارَكَ عَلَيْكَ، وَجَزَاكَ اللهُ خَيْرًا، وَرَزَقَكَ اللهُ مِثْلَهُ، وَأَجْزَلَ ثَوَابَكَ»

Baarakallahu laka wa baaraka 'alayka, wa jazaakallaahu khayran, wa razaqakallaahu mithlahu, wa 'ajzala thawaabaka.

May Allāh bless you, and shower His blessings upon you, and may Allāh reward you well and bestow upon you its like and reward you abundantly.[185]

◆

48. For seeking Allāh's protection for children

The Prophet ﷺ used to seek Allāh's protection for Al-Hasan and Al-Husain by saying:

١٤٦-«أُعِيذُكُمَا بِكَلِمَاتِ اللهِ التَّامَّةِ مِنْ كُلِّ شَيْطَانٍ وَهَامَّةٍ، وَمِنْ كُلِّ عَيْنٍ لَامَّةٍ».

’U‘eethukumaa bikalimaatil-laahit-taammati min kulli shaytaanin wa haammatin, wa min kulli ‘aynin laammatin.

I seek protection for you in the Perfect Words of Allāh from every devil and every beast, and from every envious blameworthy eye.[186]

---

185. An-Nawawi, *Kitābul-’Athkār*, p. 349, and *Sahīhul ’Athkār* 2/713 by Saleem Al-Hilāli.

186. Al-Bukhāri. 4/119.

49. When visiting the sick

«١٤٧- لَا بَأْسَ طَهُورٌ إِنْ شَاءَ اللهُ»

Laa ba'sa tahoorun 'in shaa' Allaah.

Do not worry, it will be a purification (for you), Allāh willing.[187]

- - - - - - ◆ - - - - - -

«١٤٨-أَسْأَلُ اللهَ الْعَظِيمَ رَبَّ الْعَرْشِ الْعَظِيمِ أَنْ يَشْفِيَكَ»

'As'alullaahal-'Adheema Rabbal-'Arshil-'Adheemi 'an yashfiyaka.

I ask Almighty Allāh, Lord of the Magnificent Throne, to make you well. (Recite seven times in Arabic).[188]

- - - - - - ◆ - - - - - -

---

187. Al-Bukhari, cf. Al-Asqalāni *Fathul-Bāri* 10/118.

188. At-Tirmithi, Abu Dawud. See also Al-Albāni, *Sahīh At-Tirmithi* 2/210 and *Sahīhul-Jami' As-Saghir* 5/180.

50. Reward for visiting the sick

When a man goes to visit his sick Muslim brother, he walks along a path of Paradise until he sits, and when he sits he is cloaked in mercy. If he comes in the morning, seventy thousand angels pray for him until evening, and if he comes in the evening, seventy thousand angels pray for him until morning.[189]

◆

51. For the terminally ill

١٥٠ - «اللَّهُمَّ اغْفِرْ لِي وَارْحَمْنِي وَأَلْحِقْنِي بِالرَّفِيقِ الْأَعْلَى»

Allaahum-maghfir lee warhamnee wa 'alhiqnee bir-rafeeqil-'a'laa.

O Allāh, forgive me and have mercy upon me and join me with the highest companions (in Paradise).[190]

---

189. At-Tirmithi, Ibn Mājah, Aḥmad. See Al-Albāni, *Sahīh Ibn Mājah* 1/244, and *Sahīh At-Tirmithi* 1/286. It was also graded authentic by Aḥmad Shākir.

190. Al-Bukhāri 7/10, Muslim 4/1893.

As he was dying, the Prophet ﷺ dipped his hands in water and wiped his face saying:

١٥١–«لَا إِلَهَ إِلَّا الله إِنَّ لِلْمَوْتِ لَسَكَرَاتٍ».

Laa 'ilaaha 'illallaahu 'inna lilmawti lasa-karaatin.

There is none worthy of worship but Allāh, surely death has agonies.[191]

١٥٢–لَا إِلَهَ إِلَّا الله وَاللهُ أَكْبَرُ، لَا إِلَهَ إِلَّا الله وَحْدَهُ، لَا إِلَهَ إِلَّا الله وَحْدَهُ لَا شَرِيكَ لَهُ، لَا إِلَهَ إِلَّا الله لَهُ الْمُلْكُ وَلَهُ الْحَمْدُ، لَا إِلَهَ إِلَّا الله وَلَا حَوْلَ وَلَا قُوَّةَ إِلَّا بِاللهِ»

Laa 'ilaaha 'illallaahu wallaahu 'Akbar, laa 'il-aaha 'illallaahu wahdahu, laa 'ilaaha 'illallaahu wahdahu laa shareeka lahu, laa 'ilaaha 'illallaa-hu lahul-mulku wa lahul hamdu, laa 'ilaaha 'illallaahu wa laa hawla wa laa quwwata 'illaa billaah.

---

191. Al-Bukhāri, cf. Al-Asqalāni, *Fathul-Bāri* 8 /144. The *Hadith* also mentions him using the *Siwāk* (tooth stick).

There is none worthy of worship but Allāh, Allāh is the Most Great. None has the right to be worshipped but Allāh alone. None has the right to be worshipped but Allāh alone, Who has no partner. There is none worthy of worship but Allāh, His is the dominion and His is the praise. There is none worthy of worship but Allāh, there is no power and no might but by Allāh.[192]

---

52. Encourage the dying person

«لَا إِلَهَ إِلَّا اللهُ» .

La 'ilaaha 'illallaahu.

There is none worthy of worship but Allāh.

Whoever dies with saying these last words, will enter Paradise.[193]

---

192. At-Tirmithi and Ibn Mājah. See also Al-Albāni, *Sahīh At-Tirmithi* 3/152 and *Sahīh Ibn Mājah* 2/317.
193. Abu Dawud 3/190. See also Al-Albāni, *Sahīhul-Jami' As-Saghir* 5/432.

53. When tragedy strikes

١٥٤-«إِنَّا لِلهِ وَإِنَّا إِلَيْهِ رَاجِعُونَ اللَّهُمَّ أُجُرْنِي فِي مُصِيبَتِي وَأَخْلِفْ لِي خَيْرًا مِنْهَا».

'Innaa lillaahi wa 'innaa 'ilayhi raaji'oon, Allaahumma'-jumi fee museebatee wa 'akhlif lee khayran minhaa.

We are from Allāh and unto Him we return. O Allāh take me out of my plight and bring to me after it something better.[194]

---

54. On closing the eyes of the dead

١٥٥-«اللَّهُمَّ اغْفِرْ لِفُلَانٍ (بِاسْمِهِ) وَارْفَعْ دَرَجَتَهُ فِي الْمَهْدِيِّينَ، وَاخْلُفْهُ فِي عَقِبِهِ فِي الْغَابِرِينَ، وَاغْفِرْ لَنَا وَلَهُ يَا رَبَّ الْعَالَمِينَ، وَافْسَحْ لَهُ فِي قَبْرِهِ وَنَوِّرْ لَهُ فِيهِ».

Allaahummaghfir li (name of the person) warfa' darajatahu fil-mahdiyyeena, wakhlufhu fee 'aqibihi fil-ghaabireena,

---

*waghfir-lanaa wa lahu yaa Rabbal 'aalamee-
na, wafsah lahu fee qabrihi wa nawwir lahu
feehi.*

O Allāh, forgive [name of the person] and elevate his station among those who are guided.
Send him along the path of those who came
before, and forgive us and him, O Lord of the
worlds. Enlarge for him his grave and shed
light upon him in it.[195]

---

55. For the dead's funeral prayer

١٥٦- «اللَّهُمَّ اغْفِرْ لَهُ وَارْحَمْهُ، وَعَافِهِ، وَاعْفُ عَنْهُ،
وَأَكْرِمْ نُزُلَهُ، وَوَسِّعْ مُدْخَلَهُ، وَاغْسِلْهُ بِالْمَاءِ وَالثَّلْجِ
وَالْبَرَدِ، وَنَقِّهِ مِنَ الْخَطَايَا كَمَا نَقَّيْتَ الثَّوْبَ الْأَبْيَضَ مِنَ
الدَّنَسِ، وَأَبْدِلْهُ دَارًا خَيْرًا مِنْ دَارِهِ، وَأَهْلًا خَيْرًا مِنْ
أَهْلِهِ، وَزَوْجًا خَيْرًا مِنْ زَوْجِهِ، وَأَدْخِلْهُ الْجَنَّةَ، وَأَعِذْهُ مِنْ
عَذَابِ الْقَبْرِ [وَعَذَابِ النَّارِ]».

---

195. Muslim 2/634.

*Allaahum-maghfir lahu warhamhu, wa
'aafihi, wa'fu 'anhu, wa 'akrim nuzulahu,
wa wassi' mudkhalahu, waghsilhu bilmaa'i
waththalji walbaradi, wa naqqihi minal
khataayaa kamaa naqqaytath-thawbal
'abyadha minad-danasi, wa 'abdilhu daaran
khayran min daarihi, wa 'ahlan khayran
min 'ahlihi, wa zawjan khayran min zawjihi,
wa 'adkhilhul-jannata, wa 'a'ithhu min
'athaabil-qabri [wa 'athaabin-naar].*

O Allāh, forgive him and have mercy on him
and give him strength and pardon him. Be
generous to him and cause his entrance to
be wide and wash him with water and snow
and hail. Cleanse him of his transgressions
as white cloth is cleansed of stains. Give him
an abode better than his home, and a family
better than his family and a wife better than
his wife. Take him into Paradise and protect
him from the punishment of the grave [and
from the punishment of Hell-fire].[196]

---

196. Muslim 2/663.

١٥٧-«اللَّهُمَّ اغْفِرْ لِحَيِّنَا، وَمَيِّتِنَا، وَشَاهِدِنَا، وَغَائِبِنَا،
وَصَغِيرِنَا وَكَبِيرِنَا، وَذَكَرِنَا وَأُنْثَانَا. اللَّهُمَّ مَنْ أَحْيَيْتَهُ مِنَّا
فَأَحْيِهِ عَلَى الإِسْلامِ، وَمَنْ تَوَفَّيْتَهُ مِنَّا فَتَوَفَّهُ عَلَى الإِيمَانِ،
اللَّهُمَّ لَا تَحْرِمْنَا أَجْرَهُ وَلَا تُضِلَّنَا بَعْدَهُ».

*Allaahum-maghfir lihayyinaa, wa mayyit-
inaa, wa shaahidinaa, wa ghaa'ibinaa, wa
sagheerinaa wa kabeerinaa, wa thakarinaa
wa 'unthaanaa. Allaahumma man 'ahyaytahu
minnaa fa'ahyihi 'alal 'Islaami, wa man tawaf-
faytahu minnaa fatawaffahu 'alal-'eemaani,
Allaahumma laa tahrimnaa 'ajrahu wa laa
tudhillanaa ba'dahu.*

O Allāh forgive our living and our dead, those
who are with us and those who are absent, our
young and our old, our menfolk and our wom-
enfolk. O Allāh, whomever You give life from
among us give him life in Islam, and whomever
You take way from us take him away in Faith.
O Allāh, do not forbid us their reward and do
not send us astray after them.[197]

---

197. Ibn Mājah 1/480, Aḥmad 2/368. See also Al-Albāni,
Sahīhi Ibn Mājah 1/251.

١٥٨- «اللَّهُمَّ إِنَّ فُلَانَ بْنَ فُلَانٍ فِي ذِمَّتِكَ، وَحَبْلِ
جِوَارِكَ، فَقِهِ مِنْ فِتْنَةِ الْقَبْرِ وَعَذَابِ النَّارِ، وَأَنْتَ أَهْلُ
الْوَفَاءِ وَالْحَقِّ. فَاغْفِرْ لَهُ وَارْحَمْهُ إِنَّكَ أَنْتَ الْغَفُورُ
الرَّحِيمُ».

Allaahumma 'inna [name the person] fee thimmatika, wa habli jiwaarika, faqihi min fitnatil-qabri wa 'athaabin-naari, wa 'Anta 'ahlul-wafaa'i walhaqqi. Faghfir lahu warhamhu 'innaka 'Antal-Ghafoorur-Raheem.

O Allāh, surely *[name the person]* is under Your protection, and in the rope of Your security, so save him from the trial of the grave and from the punishment of the Fire. You fulfill promises and grant rights, so forgive him and have mercy on him. Surely You are Most Forgiving, Most Merciful.[198]

◆

---

198. Ibn Mājah, Abu Dawud 3/211. See also Al-Albāni, *Sahīhi Ibn Mājah* 1/251.

١٥٩-«اللَّهُمَّ عَبْدُكَ وَابْنُ أَمَتِكَ احْتَاجَ إِلَى رَحْمَتِكَ، وَأَنْتَ غَنِيٌّ عَنْ عَذَابِهِ، إِنْ كَانَ مُحْسِنًا فَزِدْ فِي حَسَنَاتِهِ، وَإِنْ كَانَ مُسِيئًا فَتَجَاوَزْ عَنْهُ».

Allaahumma 'abduka wabnu 'amatika ihtaaja 'ilaa rahmatika, wa 'Anta ghaniyyun 'an 'athaabihi, 'in kaana muhsinan fazid fee hasanaatihi, wa 'in kaana musee'an fatajaawaz 'anhu.

O Allāh, Your male slave and the child of Your female slave is in need of Your mercy, and You are not in need of his torment. If he was pious then increase his rewards and if he was a transgressor then pardon him.[199]

- - - - - - - - ◆ - - - - - - - -

---

199. Al-Hākim 1/359 who graded it authentic and Ath-Thahabi agreed with him. See also Al-Albāni, *Ahkamul-Janā'iz*, p. 125.

56. For a child's Funeral prayer

١٦٠-«اللَّهُمَّ أَعِذْهُ مِنْ عَذَابِ الْقَبْرِ» وَإِنْ قَالَ: «اللَّهُمَّ
اجْعَلْهُ فَرَطًا وَذُخْرًا لِوَالِدَيْهِ، وَشَفِيعًا مُجَابًا. اللَّهُمَّ ثَقِّلْ بِهِ
مَوَازِينَهُمَا وَأَعْظِمْ بِهِ أُجُورَهُمَا، وَأَلْحِقْهُ بِصَالِحِ
الْمُؤْمِنِينَ، وَاجْعَلْهُ فِي كَفَالَةِ إِبْرَاهِيمَ، وَقِهِ بِرَحْمَتِكَ
عَذَابَ الْجَحِيمِ، وَأَبْدِلْهُ دَارًا خَيْرًا مِنْ دَارِهِ، وَأَهْلًا خَيْرًا
مِنْ أَهْلِهِ، اللَّهُمَّ غْفِرْ لِأَسْلَافِنَا وَأَفْرَاطِنَا، وَمَنْ سَبَقَنَا بِالْإِيمَانِ».

Allaahumma 'a'ith-hu min 'athaabil qabri.
[or say:] *Allaahum-maj'alhu faratan wa*
thukhran liwaalidayhi, wa shafee'an mujaaban.
Allaahumma thaqqil bihi mawaazeenahumaa
wa 'a'dhim bihi 'ujoorahumaa, wa 'alhiqhu
bisaalihil-mu'mineena, waj'alhu fee kafaalati
'Ibraaheema, wa qihi birahmatika 'athaa-
bal-jaheemi, wa 'abdilhu daaran khayran min
daarihi, wa 'ahlan khayran min 'ahlihi, Allaa-
hum-maghfir li'aslaafinaa, wa 'afraatinaa wa
man sabaqanaa bil'eemaan.

O Allāh, protect him from the torment of the
grave. [It is also good to say:] O Allāh, make

him a precursor, a forerunner and a treasure for his parents and an answered intercessor. O Allāh, make him weigh heavily in their scales (of good) and magnify their reward. Make him join the righteous of the believers. Place him in the care of Ibrahim. Save him by Your mercy from the torment of Hell. Give him a home better than his home and a family better than his family. O Allāh, forgive those who have gone (i.e. passed away) before us, our children lost (by death), and those who have preceded us in Faith.[200]

---•---

١٦١ –«اللَّهُمَّ اجْعَلْهُ لَنَا فَرَطًا، وَسَلَفًا، وَأَجْرًا».

Allaahum-maj'alhu lanaa faratan, wa salafan, wa 'ajran.

O Allāh, make him for us a precursor, a fore-runner and a cause of reward.[201]

---

200. Ibn Qudāmah, Al-Mughni 3/416 and *Ad-Duroosul-Muhimmah li-'Aammatil-'Ummah*, p. 15, by Shaikh 'Abdul-'Aziz bin Bāz.

201. Al-Hasan (Al-Basri) used to recite *Surat Al-Fātihah* for a child's funeral and then say the above. Al-Bukhari, *Kitābul Janā'iz*, p. 65.

57. For the bereaved

١٦٢-«إِنَّ لِلَّهِ مَا أَخَذَ، وَلَهُ مَا أَعْطَى وَكُلُّ شَيْءٍ عِنْدَهُ بِأَجَلٍ مُسَمًّى... فَلْتَصْبِرْ وَلْتَحْتَسِبْ».

'Inna lillaahi maa 'akhatha, wa lahu maa 'a'taa, wa kullu shay'in 'indahu bi'ajalin musamman... faltasbir waltahtasib.

Surely, Allāh takes what is His, and what He gives is His, and to all things He has appointed a time... so have patience and be rewarded.[202]

Also good to say:

«أَعْظَمَ اللهُ أَجْرَكَ، وَأَحْسَنَ عَزَاءَكَ وَغَفَرَ لِمَيِّتِكَ».

'A 'dhamallaahu 'ajraka, wa 'ahsana 'azaa'aka wa ghafara limayyitika.

May Allāh magnify your reward, and make perfect your bereavement, and forgive your departed.[203]

---

202. Al-Bukhāri 2/80, Muslim 2/636.

203. An-Nawawi, Kitabul-'Athkar, p.126.

58. When placing the dead in the grave

١٦٣ - «بِسْمِ اللهِ وَعَلَى سُنَّةِ رَسُولِ اللهِ».

Bismillaahi wa 'alaa sunnati Rasoolillaahi.

With the Name of Allāh and according to the *Sunnah* of the Messenger of Allāh.[204]

---

59. After burying the dead

١٦٤ - «اللَّهُمَّ اغْفِرْ لَهُ اللَّهُمَّ ثَبِّتْهُ».

Allaahum-maghfir lahu Allaahumma thabbithu.

O Allāh, forgive him. O Allāh, strengthen him.[205]

---

204. Abu Dawud 3/314 with an authentic chain. Aḥmad also recorded it with the wording: With the Name of Allāh, and according to the religion of the Messenger of Allāh. Its chain is also authentic.

205. The Prophet ﷺ used to stop after burying the dead and say to the people: "Ask Allāh to forgive your brother and pray for him to be strengthened, for indeed he is now being questioned." Abu Dawud 3/315, and Al-Ḥākim 1/370 who graded it authentic and Aṯ-Ṯhahabi agreed.

60. At the graves

١٦٥ - «السَّلَامُ عَلَيْكُمْ أَهْلَ الدِّيَارِ، مِنَ الْمُؤْمِنِينَ وَالْمُسْلِمِينَ، وَإِنَّا إِنْ شَاءَ اللهُ بِكُمْ لَاحِقُونَ [وَيَرْحَمُ اللهُ الْمُسْتَقْدِمِينَ مِنَّا وَالْمُسْتَأْخِرِينَ] أَسْأَلُ اللهَ لَنَا وَلَكُمُ الْعَافِيَةَ».

Assalaamu 'alaykum 'ahlad-diyaari, minal-mu'mineena walmuslimeena, wa 'innaa 'in shaa' Allaahu bikum laahiqoona, [wa yarha-mullaahul-mustaqdimeena minnaa walmusta'khireena] 'as'alullaaha lanaa wa lakumul-'aafiyata.

Peace be upon you, people of this abode, from among the believers and those who are Muslims, and we, by the Will of Allāh, shall be joining you. [May Allāh have mercy on the first of us and the last of us] I ask Allāh to grant us and you strength.[206]

---

206. Muslim 2/671, Ibn Mājah 1/494, the portion in brackets is from Muslim 2/671.

61. When the wind blows

١٦٦–«اللَّهُمَّ إِنِّي أَسْأَلُكَ خَيْرَهَا ، وَأَعُوذُ بِكَ مِنْ شَرِّهَا» .

Allaahumma 'innee 'as'aluka khayrahaa, wa 'a'oothu bika min sharrihaa.

O Allāh, I ask You for the good of it and seek refuge in You against its evil.[207]

•

١٦٧–«اللَّهُمَّ إِنِّي أَسْأَلُكَ خَيْرَهَا ، وَخَيْرَ مَا فِيهَا ، وَخَيْرَ مَا أُرْسِلَتْ بِهِ وَأَعُوذُ بِكَ مِنْ شَرِّهَا ، وَشَرِّ مَا فِيهَا ، وَشَرِّ مَا أُرْسِلَتْ بِهِ» .

Allaahumma 'innee 'as'aluka khayrahaa, wa khayra maa feehaa, wa khayra maa 'ursilat bihi wa 'a'oothu bika min sharrihaa, wa sharri maa feehaa, wa sharri maa 'ursilat bihi.

O Allāh, I ask You for the good of it, for the

---

207. Dawud 4/326, Ibn Mājah 2/1228. See also Al-Albāni, *Sahīh Ibn Mājah* 2/305.

good of what it contains, and for the good of what is sent with it. I seek refuge in You from the evil of it, from the evil of what it contains, and from the evil that is sent with it.[208]

* * *

62. When it thunders

١٦٨ -«سُبْحَانَ الَّذِي يُسَبِّحُ الرَّعْدُ بِحَمْدِهِ وَالْمَلَائِكَةُ مِنْ خِيفَتِهِ».

Subhaanal-lathee yusabbihur-ra'du bihamdi-hi walmalaa'ikatu min kheefatihi.

Glory is to Him Whom thunder and angels glorify due to fear of Him.[209]

---

208. Muslim 2/616, Al-Bukhāri 4/76.

209. Whenever Abdullah bin Zubair would hear thunder, he would abandon all conversation and say this supplication. See *Al-Muwatta'* 2/992. It was graded authentic by Al-Albāni as a statement of Abdullah bin Zubayr only.

63. For having rain

١٦٩ -«اللَّهُمَّ أَسْقِنَا غَيْثًا مُغِيثًا مَرِيئًا مَرِيعًا، نَافِعًا غَيْرَ ضَارٍّ، عَاجِلًا غَيْرَ آجِلٍ».

Allaahumma 'asqinaa ghaythan mugheethan maree'an maree'an, naafi'an ghayra dhaarrin, 'aajilan ghayra 'aajilin.

O Allāh, shower upon us abundant rain, beneficial, not harmful, swiftly and not delayed.[210]

--------------- • ---------------

١٧٠ -«اللَّهُمَّ أَغِثْنَا، اللَّهُمَّ أَغِثْنَا، اللَّهُمَّ أَغِثْنَا».

Allaahumma 'aghithnaa, Allaahumma 'aghithnaa, Allaahumma 'aghithnaa.

O Allāh, send us rain. O Allāh, send us rain. O Allāh, send us rain.[211]

---

210. Abu Dawud 1/ 303. See also Al-Albāni SahīhAbu Dawud 1/216.

211. Al-Bukhāri 1/224, Muslim 2/613.

١٧١ –«اللَّهُمَّ اسْقِ عِبَادَكَ، وَبَهَائِمَكَ، وَانْشُرْ رَحْمَتَكَ، وَأَحْيِ بَلَدَكَ الْمَيِّتَ».

Allaahum-masqi 'ibaadaka, wa bahaa'im-aka, wanshur rahmataka, wa 'ahyi balada-kal-mayyita.

O Allāh, give water to Your slaves, and Your livestock, and spread Your mercy, and revive Your dead land.[212]

◆

---

64. When it rains

١٧٢ –«اللَّهُمَّ صَيِّبًا نَافِعًا».

Allaahumma sayyiban naafi'an.

O Allāh, (bring) beneficial rain clouds.[213]

---

212. Abu Dawud 1/305. Al-Albāni graded it good in *SahīhAbuDawud* 1/218.

213. Al-Bukhāri, cf. Al-Asqalāni, *Fathul-Bāri* 2/518.

65. After it rains

١٧٣ –«مُطِرْنَا بِفَضْلِ اللهِ وَرَحْمَتِهِ».

Mutirnaa bifadhlillaahi wa rahmatihi.

It has rained by the bounty of Allāh and His mercy.[214]

---

66. To withhold the rain

١٧٤ –«اللَّهُمَّ حَوَالَيْنَا وَلَا عَلَيْنَا. اللَّهُمَّ عَلَى الآكَامِ وَالظِّرَابِ، وَبُطُونِ الأَوْدِيَةِ، وَمَنَابِتِ الشَّجَرِ».

Allaahumma hawaalaynaa wa laa 'alaynaa. Allaahumma 'alal-'aakaami wa<u>dh-db</u>-iraabi, wa butoonil-'awdiyati, wa manaabitish-shajari.

O Allāh, let it pass us and not fall upon us, but upon the hills and mountains, and the center of the valleys, and upon the forested lands.[215]

---

214. Al-Bukhāri 1/205, Muslim 1/83.
215. Al-Bukhāri 1/224, Muslim 1/614.

67. On sighting the new moon

١٧٥-«اللهُ أَكْبَرُ، اللَّهُمَّ أَهِلَّهُ عَلَيْنَا بِالأَمْنِ وَالإِيمَانِ،
وَالسَّلامَةِ وَالإِسْلامِ، وَالتَّوْفِيقِ لِمَا تُحِبُّ رَبَّنَا وَتَرْضَى،
رَبُّنَا وَرَبُّكَ اللهُ».

*Allaahu 'Akbar, Allaahumma 'ahillahu
'alayna bil'amni wal'eemaani, wassalaama-
ti wal-'Islaami, wattawfeeqi limaa tuhibbu
Rabbanaa wa tardhaa, Rabbunaa wa Rab-
bukallaahu.*

Allāh is the Most Great. O Allāh, bring us the
new moon with security and Faith, with peace
and in Islam, and in harmony with what our
Lord loves and what pleases Him. Our Lord
and your Lord is Allāh.[216]

---------------◆---------------

---

216. At-Tirmithi 5/504, Ad-Darimi 1/336. See also Al-
     Albāni, *Sahīh At-Tirmithi* 57.

68. For breaking the fast

١٧٦- «ذَهَبَ الظَّمَأُ وَابْتَلَّتِ الْعُرُوقُ، وَثَبَتَ الْأَجْرُ إِنْ شَاءَ اللهُ».

Thahabadh-dhama'u wabtallatil 'urooqu, wa thabatal-'ajru 'in shaa' Allaah.

The thirst is gone, the veins are moistened and the reward is confirmed, if Allāh wills.[217]

١٧٧- «اللَّهُمَّ إِنِّي أَسْأَلُكَ بِرَحْمَتِكَ الَّتِي وَسِعَتْ كُلَّ شَيْءٍ أَنْ تَغْفِرَ لِي».

Allaahumma 'innee 'as'aluka birahmatikal-la-tee wasi'at kulla shay'in 'an taghfira lee.

O Allāh, I ask You by Your mercy, which encompasses all things, that You forgive me.[218]

---

217. Abu Dawud 2/306 and others. See also Al-Albāni, _Sahīhul-Jami' As-Saghir_ 4/209.

218. Ibn Mājah 1/557 from a supplication of Abdullah bin 'Amr. Al-Hāfidh graded it as good in his checking of An-Nawawi's _Kitabul-'Athkār_. See _Sharhul-'Athkār_ 4/342.

69. Before eating

When you begin eating, say:

«بِسْمِ اللهِ» .

Bismillaah. With the Name of Allāh.

If you forget, then when you remember, say:

«بِسْمِ اللهِ فِي أَوَّلِهِ وَآخِرِهِ» .

Bismillaahifee 'awwalihi wa 'aakhirihi.

With the Name of Allāh, in the beginning and in the end.[219]

•

Whomever Allāh has given food, should say:

«اللَّهُمَّ بَارِكْ لَنَا فِيهِ وَأَطْعِمْنَا خَيْرًا مِنْهُ» .

---

219. Abu Dawud 3/347, At-Tirmithi 4/288.
See Al-Albāni's *Sahīh At-Tirmithi* 2/167.

Allaahumma baarik lanaafeehi wa 'at'imnaa khayran minhu.

O Allāh, bless us in it and provide us with better than it.

━━━━━ ◆ ━━━━━

Whomever Allāh has given milk to drink, should say:

«اللَّهُمَّ بَارِكْ لَنَا فِيهِ وَزِدْنَا مِنْهُ».

Allaahumma baarik lanaa feehi wa zidnaa minhu.

O Allāh, bless us in it and give us more of it.[220]

━━━━━ ◆ ━━━━━

220. At-Tirmithi 5/506. See also Al-Albāni, *Sahīh At-Tirmithi* 158.

70. After eating

١٨٠-«الْحَمْدُ لله الَّذي أَطْعَمَني هَذَا، وَرَزَقَنيهِ، مِنْ غَيْرِ حَوْلٍ مِنِّي وَلَا قُوَّةٍ».

Alhamdu lillaahil-lathee 'at'amanee haathaa, wa razaqaneehi, min ghayri hawlin minnee wa laa quwwatin.

Praise is to Allāh Who has given me this food and sustained me with it though I was unable to do it and powerless.[221]

------------◆------------

١٨١-«الْحَمْدُ لله حَمْدًا كَثيرًا طَيِّبًا مُبَارَكًا فيهِ، غَيْرَ [مَكْفيٍّ وَلَا] مُوَدَّعٍ، وَلَا مُسْتَغْنًى عَنْهُ رَبَّنَا».

Alhamdu lillaahi hamdan katheeran tayyiban mubaarakan feehi, ghayra [makfiyyin wa laa] muwadda'in, wa laa mustaghnan 'anhu Rabbanaa.

---

221. At-Tirmi<u>th</u>i, Abu Dawud, and Ibn Mājah. See also Al-Albāni, *Sahīh At-Tirmithi* 3/159.

All praise is to Allāh, praise in abundance, good and blessed. It cannot (be compensated for, nor can it) be left, nor can it be done without, our Lord.[222]

71. From a dinner guest for his host

١٨٢-«اللَّهُمَّ بَارِكْ لَهُمْ فِيمَا رَزَقْتَهُمْ، وَاغْفِرْ لَهُمْ وَارْحَمْهُمْ».

Allaahumma baarik lahum feemaa razaqtahum, waghfir lahum warhamhum.

O Allāh, bless them in what You have provided for them, and forgive them and have mercy on them.[223]

---

222. Al-Bukhāri 6/214, At-Tirmithi 5/507.
223. Muslim 3/1615.

72. For one who offers you a drink

١٨٣ -«اللَّهُمَّ أَطْعِمْ مَنْ أَطْعَمَنِي وَاسْقِ مَنْ سَقَانِي».

Allaahumma 'at'im man 'at'amanee wasqi man saqaanee.

O Allāh, feed the one who has fed me and give drink to the one who has given me drink.[224]

✦

73. For a family who invites you to break your fast

١٨٤ -«أَفْطَرَ عِنْدَكُمُ الصَّائِمُونَ، وَأَكَلَ طَعَامَكُمُ الْأَبْرَارُ، وَصَلَّتْ عَلَيْكُمُ الْمَلَائِكَةُ».

'Aftara 'indakumus-saa'imoona, wa 'akala ta'aamakumul-'abraaru, wa sallat 'alayku-mul-malaa'ikatu.

With you, those who are fasting have broken their fast, you have fed those who are righteous,

---

224. Muslim 3/126.

and the angels recite their prayers upon you.[225]

◆

74. For one who offers you food when you are fasting, but you decline

When you are invited (to eat) then reply to the invitation. If you are fasting then invoke Allāh's blessings (on your host), and if you are not fasting then eat.[226]

◆

75. When you are fasting and someone is rude to you

١٨٦ –«إِنِّي صَائِمٌ، إِنِّي صَائِمٌ».

'Innee saa'imun, 'innee saa'imun.

I am fasting. I am fasting.[227]

---

225. Abu Dawud 3/367, Ibn Mājah 1/556, An-Nasā'i, 'Amalul-Yawm wal-Laylah 296-8. Al-Albāni graded it authentic in Sahīh Abu Dawud 2/730.

226. Muslim 2/1054.

227. Al-Bukhāri, cf. Al-Asqalāni, Fathul-Bāri 4/103, Muslim 2/806.

76. When you see the first dates of the season

١٨٧ -«اللَّهُمَّ بَارِكْ لَنَا فِي ثَمَرِنَا، وَبَارِكْ لَنَا فِي مَدِينَتِنَا وَبَارِكْ لَنَا فِي صَاعِنَا، وَبَارِكْ لَنَا فِي مُدِّنَا».

Allahumma baarik lanaa fee thamarinaa, wa baarik lanaa fee madeenatinaa wa baarik lanaa fee saa'inaa, wa baarik lanaa fee mud-dinaa.

O Allāh, bless us in our dates and bless us in our town, bless us in our *Sā'* and in our *Mudd*.[228]

---

228. Muslim 2/1000 (*Sā'* and *Mudd* are both dry measures used for agricultural produce by the Arabs in the Prophet's ﷺ time. Of the two, the *Sā'* was the larger measure.) (Translator).

77. After sneezing

When you sneeze, say:

«الْحَمْدُ لِلَّهِ».

Alhamdu lillaah.

All praises and thanks are to Allāh.

Your companion should say:

«يَرْحَمُكَ اللهُ».

Yarhamukallaah.

May Allāh have mercy upon you.

When someone says *Yarhamukallaah* to you, then you should say:

«يَهْدِيكُمُ اللهُ وَيُصْلِحُ بَالَكُمْ».

Yahdeekumul-laahu wa yuslihu baalakum.

May Allāh guide you and set your affairs in order. [229]

-------------- ◆ --------------

229. Al-Bukhāri 7/125.

78. For the disbeliever if he sneezes and praises Allāh

١٨٩ - «يَهْدِيكُمُ اللهُ وَيُصْلِحُ بَالَكُمْ».

Yahdeekumullaahu wa yuslihu baalakum.

May Allāh guide you and set your affairs in order.[230]

◆

79. For the groom

١٩٠ - «بَارَكَ اللهُ لَكَ، وَبَارَكَ عَلَيْكَ؛ وَجَمَعَ بَيْنَكُمَا فِي خَيْرٍ».

Baarakallaahu laka, wa baaraka 'alayka, wa jama'a baynakumaa fee khayrin.

May Allāh bless you, and shower His blessings upon you, and join you together in goodness.[231]

---

230. At-Tirmithi 5/82, Aḥmad 4/400, AbuDawud 4/308. See also Al-Albāni, *Sahīh At-Tirmithi* 2/354.

231. Abu Dawud, Ibn Mājah and At-Tirmithi. See also Al-Albani, *Sahīh At-Tirmithi* 1/ 316.

80. For the groom and upon purchasing an animal

When any of you marry a woman or purchase a maid-servant then say:

١٩١-«اللّهُمَّ إِنِّي أَسْأَلُكَ خَيْرَهَا وَخَيْرَ مَا جَبَلْتَهَا عَلَيْهِ وَأَعُوذُ بِكَ مِنْ شَرِّهَا وَشَرِّ مَا جَبَلْتَهَا عَلَيْهِ».

Allaahumma 'innee 'as'aluka khayrahaa wa khayra ma jabaltahaa 'alayhi wa 'a'oothu bika min sharrihaa wa sharri maajabaltahaa 'alayhi.

O Allāh, I ask You for the goodness of her and the goodness upon which You have created her, and I seek refuge in You from the evil of her and from the evil upon which You have created her.

If you purchase a camel then take hold of the top of its hump and say the same.[232]

---

232. Abu Dawud 2/248 and Ibn Mājah 1/617.
    See also Al-Albani, *Sahīh Ibn Mājah* 1/324.

81. Before having an intercourse

١٩٢ -«بِسْمِ اللهِ. اللَّهُمَّ جَنِّبْنَا الشَّيْطَانَ، وَجَنِّبِ الشَّيْطَانَ مَا رَزَقْتَنَا».

Bismillaah. Allaahumma jannibnash Shaytaana-na, wa jannibish-Shaytaana maa razaqtanaa.

With the Name of Allāh. O Allāh, keep the Devil away from us and keep the Devil away from that which You provide for us.[233]

━━━━━━ • ━━━━━━

82. Against anger

١٩٣ -«أَعُوذُ بِاللهِ مِنَ الشَّيْطَانِ الرَّجِيمِ».

'Aoothu billaahi minash-Shaytaanir rajeem.

I seek refuge in Allāh from Satan the outcast.[234]

---

233. Al-Bukhāri 6/141, Muslim 2/1028.
234. Al-Bukhāri 7/99, Muslim 4/2015.

83. When someone is afflicted with misfortune

١٩٤-«الْحَمْدُ للهِ الَّذِي عَافَانِي مِمَّا ابْتَلَاكَ بِهِ وَفَضَّلَنِي
عَلَى كَثِيرٍ مِمَّنْ خَلَقَ تَفْضِيلًا».

Alhamdu lillaahil-lathee 'aafaanee mimmab-talaaka bihi wa fadhdhalanee 'alaa katheerin mimman khalaqa tafdheela.

Praise is to Allāh Who has spared me what He has afflicted you with, and preferred me greatly above much of what He has created.[235]

- - - - - - - - ◆ - - - - - - - -

84. While sitting in an assembly

Ibn Umar ﷺ said: Allāh's Messenger ﷺ used to repeat in a single sitting:

١٩٥-رَبِّ اغْفِرْ لِي وَتُبْ عَلَيَّ إِنَّكَ أَنْتَ التَّوَّابُ الْغَفُورُ».

---

235. At-Tirmithi 5/493,4. See also Al-Albāni, *Sahih At-Tirmithi* 3/153.

Rabbighfir lee wa tub 'alayya 'innaka 'Antat-Tawwaabul-Ghafoor.

My Lord, forgive me and accept my repentance, You are the Ever-Relenting, the All-Forgiving.[236]

◆

85. For Expiation of Assembly – *Kaffâratul-Majlis*

١٩٦-«سُبْحَانَكَ اللَّهُمَّ وَبِحَمْدِكَ، أَشْهَدُ أَنْ لَا إِلَهَ إِلَّا أَنْتَ، أَسْتَغْفِرُكَ وَأَتُوبُ إِلَيْكَ».

Subhaanaka Allaahumma wa bihamdika, 'ashhadu 'an laa 'ilaaha 'illaa 'Anta, 'astaghfiruka wa 'atoobu 'ilayka.

Glory is to You, O Allāh, and praise is to You. I bear witness that there is none worthy of worship but You. I seek Your forgiveness and repent to You.[237]

---

236. *Sahīh Ibn Mājah* 2/321. See also Al-Albāni, *Sahīh At-Tirmithi* 3/153.

237. Abu Dawud, Ibn Mājah, At-Tirmithi and An Nasā'i. See also Al-Albāni, *Sahīh At-Tirmithi* 3/153. Aishah

86. Replying someone who says: "May Allāh forgive you."

١٩٧ - «وَلَكَ» .

Walaka. And you.[238]

--------------◆--------------

87. For one who does good to you

١٩٨ - «جَزَاكَ اللهُ خَيْرًا» .

Jazaakallaahu khayran.

May Allāh reward you with good.[239]

رضي الله عنه said: "Allāh's Messenger ﷺ did not sit in a gathering, and did not recite the Qur'ān, and did not perform any prayer without concluding by saying... (then she quoted the above)." This was reported by An-Nasā'i in *'Amalul-Yawm wal-Laylah* (no. 308), and Dr. Farooq Hamādah graded it authentic in his checking of the same book, p. 273. See also Aḥmad 6/77.

238. Aḥmad 5/82, and An-Nasā'i in *'Amalul-Yawm wal-Laylah* p. 218, with checking by Dr. Farooq Hamādah.

239. At-Tirmithi (no. 2035). See also Al-Albāni, *Saḥīḥ At-Tirmithi* 2/200 and *Saḥīḥul-Jami'* (no. 6244).

88. Seeking Allāh's protection from the False Messiah

Whoever memorizes ten 'Āyat (Verses) from the beginning of *Surat Al-Kahf*, will be protected from the False Messiah.[240] He should also seek refuge in Allah from him in every prayer after the final *Tashahhud* before ending the prayer.[241]

◆

89. For someone who tells you: "I love you for the sake of Allāh."

٢٠٠-«أَحَبَّكَ الَّذِي أَحْبَبْتَنِي لَهُ»

'Ahabbakal-lathee 'ahbabtanee lahu.

May He, for Whose sake you love me, love you.[242]

---

240. Muslim 1/555, another version mentions the last ten *āyat*, Muslim 1/556.

241. See page 54 and 55.

242. Abu Dawud 4/333. Al-Albāni graded it good in *Sahīh Abu Dawud* 3/965.

90. For someone who offers you a share of his wealth

٢٠١-«بَارَكَ اللهُ لَكَ فِي أَهْلِكَ وَمَالِكَ».

Baarakallaahu laka fee 'ahlika wa maalika.

May Allāh bless you in your family and your property.[243]

◆

91. For one who lends you money (upon receipt of the loan)

٢٠٢-«بَارَكَ اللهُ لَكَ فِي أَهْلِكَ وَمَالِكَ، إِنَّمَا جَزَاءُ السَّلَفِ الْحَمْدُ وَالْأَدَاءُ».

Baarakallaahu laka fee 'ahlika wa maalika, 'innamaa jazaa'us-salafil-hamdu wal'adaa'.

May Allāh bless you in your family and your

---

243. Al-Bukhāri, cf. Al-Asqalāni, *Fathul-Bāri* 4/ 88.

wealth surely the reward for a loan is praise and returning (what was borrowed).[244]

◆

92. For fear of *Shirk*

٢٠٣-«اللَّهُمَّ إِنِّي أَعُوذُ بِكَ أَنْ أُشْرِكَ بِكَ وَأَنَا أَعْلَمُ، وَأَسْتَغْفِرُكَ لِمَا لَا أَعْلَمُ».

Allaahumma 'innee 'a'oothu bika 'an 'ushri-ka bika wa 'anaa 'a'lamu, wa 'astaghfiruka limaa laa 'a'lamu.

O Allāh, I seek refuge in You lest I associate anything with You knowingly, and I seek Your forgiveness for what I know not.[245]

---

244. An-Nasā'i, *'Amalul-Yawm wal-Laylah* p. 300, Ibn Mājah 2/809. See also Al-Albāni, *Sahīh Ibn Mājah* 2/55.

245. Ahmad 4/403. Seealso Al-Albāni, *Sahīhul-Jāmi' As-Saghir* 3/233 and *Sahīhut-Targhīb wat-Tarhīb* 1/19.

93. For someone who tells you: "May Allâh bless you."

٢٠٤-«وَفِيكَ بَارَكَ اللهُ».

Wa feeka baarakallaahu.

And may Allāh bless you.[246]

◆

94. Against evil portent

٢٠٥-«اللَّهُمَّ لَا طَيْرَ إِلَّا طَيْرُكَ، وَلَا خَيْرَ إِلَّا خَيْرُكَ، وَلَا إِلَهَ غَيْرُكَ».

Allaahumma laa tayra 'illaa tayruka, wa laa khayra 'illaa khayruka, wa laa 'ilaaha ghayruka.

O Allāh there is no portent other than Your portent, no goodness other than Your good

---

246. Ibn As-Sunni, p. 138, (no. 278). See also Ibn Al-Qayyim, *Al-Wābil As-Sayyib*, p. 304, with checking by Basheer Muhammad 'Uyoon.

ness, and none worthy of worship other
than You.[247]

---------------- ◆ ----------------

95. For riding a vehicle or on an animal

٢٠٦ - بِسْمِ اللهِ، الْحَمْدُ للهِ ﴿سُبْحَانَ ٱلَّذِى سَخَّرَ لَنَا هَٰذَا
وَمَا كُنَّا لَهُ مُقْرِنِينَ ۝ وَإِنَّا إِلَىٰ رَبِّنَا لَمُنقَلِبُونَ﴾ الْحَمْدُ للهِ،
الْحَمْدُ للهِ، الْحَمْدُ للهِ، اللهُ أَكْبَرُ، اللهُ أَكْبَرُ، اللهُ أَكْبَرُ،
سُبْحَانَكَ اللَّهُمَّ إِنِّي ظَلَمْتُ نَفْسِي فَاغْفِرْ لِي، فَإِنَّهُ لَا يَغْفِرُ
الذُّنُوبَ إِلَّا أَنْتَ».

Bismillaah, Alhamdu lillaah.
Subhaanal-lathee sakhkhara lanaa haathaa

----

247. Aḥmad 2/220, Ibn As-Sunni (no. 292).
See also Al-Albānī, *Silsilatul-'Aḥādīth As-Saḥīḥah*
3/54, (no. 1065). As for bodings of good, these
used to please the Prophet ﷺ and so when he heard
good words from someone, he used to say: "We
have taken from you a good portent from your
mouth," Abu Dawud, Aḥmad. See also Al-Albānī,
Silsilatul-'Aḥādīth As-Saḥīḥah 2/363, and it is with
Abu Ash-Shaikh Al-Asfahānī in *'Akhlāqun Nabiyy*,
p. 270.

*wa maa kunnaa lahu muqrineen. Wa 'innaa
'ilaa Rabbinaa lamunqaliboon. Alhamdu
lillaah, alhamdu lillaah, alhamdu lillaah,
Allaahu 'Akbar, Allaahu 'Akbar, Allaahu
'Akbar, subhaanakal-laahumma 'innee
dhalamtu nafsee faghfir lee, fa'innahu laa
yaghfiruth-thunooba 'illaa 'Anta.*

With the Name of Allāh. Praise is to Allāh.
Glory is to Him Who has provided this for us
though we could never have had it by our efforts. Surely, unto our Lord we are returning.
Praise is to Allāh. Praise is to Allāh. Praise is
to Allāh. Allāh is the Most Great. Allāh is the
Most Great. Allāh is the Most Great. Glory
is to You. O Allāh, I have wronged my own
soul. Forgive me, for surely none forgives sins
but You.[248]

---

248. Abu Dawud 3/34, At-Tirmithi 5/501. See also
Al-Albāni, *Sahīh At-Tirmithi* 3/156.

96. When traveling

٢٠٧-اللّٰهُ أَكْبَرُ، اللّٰهُ أَكْبَرُ، اللّٰهُ أَكْبَرُ، ﴿سُبْحَانَ الَّذِي سَخَّرَ لَنَا هَذَا وَمَا كُنَّا لَهُ مُقْرِنِينَ ۝ وَإِنَّا إِلَى رَبِّنَا لَمُنْقَلِبُونَ﴾ اللّٰهُمَّ إِنَّا نَسْأَلُكَ فِي سَفَرِنَا هَذَا الْبِرَّ وَالتَّقْوَى، وَمِنَ الْعَمَلِ مَا تَرْضَى، اللّٰهُمَّ هَوِّنْ عَلَيْنَا سَفَرَنَا هَذَا وَاطْوِ عَنَّا بُعْدَهُ، اللّٰهُمَّ أَنْتَ الصَّاحِبُ فِي السَّفَرِ، وَالْخَلِيفَةُ فِي الْأَهْلِ، اللّٰهُمَّ إِنِّي أَعُوذُ بِكَ مِنْ وَعْثَاءِ السَّفَرِ، وَكَآبَةِ الْمَنْظَرِ، وَسُوءِ الْمُنْقَلَبِ، فِي الْمَالِ وَالْأَهْلِ».

Allaahu 'Akbar, Allaahu 'Akbar, Allaahu 'Akbar, Subhaanal- lathee sakhkhara lanaa haathaa wa maa kunnaa lahu muqrineen. Wa 'innaa 'ilaa Rabbinaa lamun qaliboon. Allaahumma 'innaa nas'aluka fee safarinaa haathal-birra wat-taqwaa, waminal-'amali-maa tardhaa, Allaahumma hawwin 'alaynaa safaranaa haathaa watwi 'annaa bu'dahu, Allaahumma 'Antas-saahibu fis-safari, walkhaleefatu fil-'ahli, Allaahumma 'innee 'a'oothu bika min wa'thaa'is-safari, wa ka'aabatil-mandhari, wa soo'il-munqalabi fil maaliwal 'ahli.

Allāh is the Most Great. Allāh is the Most Great. Allāh is the Mos t Great. Glory is to Him Who has provided this for us though we could never have had it by our efforts. Surely, unto our Lord we are returning. O Allāh, we ask You on this our journey for goodness and piety, and for works that are pleasing to You. O Allāh, lighten this journey for us and make its distance easy for us. O Allāh, You are our Companion on the road and the One in Whose care we leave our family. O Allāh, I seek refuge in You from this journey's hardships, and from the wicked sights in store and from finding our family and property in misfortune upon returning.

(Upon returning recite the same again adding:)

«آيِبُونَ، تَائِبُونَ، عَابِدُونَ، لِرَبِّنَا حَامِدُونَ».

'Aa'iboona, taa'iboona, 'aabidoona, lirabbin-aa haamidoon.

We return repentant to our Lord, worshipping our Lord, and praising our Lord.[249]

---

249. Muslim 2/978.

97. When entering a town or city

٢٠٨-«اللَّهُمَّ رَبَّ السَّمٰوَاتِ السَّبْعِ وَمَا أَظْلَلْنَ، وَرَبَّ
الْأَرَضِينَ السَّبْعِ وَمَا أَقْلَلْنَ، وَرَبَّ الشَّيَاطِينِ وَمَا أَضْلَلْنَ،
وَرَبَّ الرِّيَاحِ وَمَا ذَرَيْنَ. أَسْأَلُكَ خَيْرَ هٰذِهِ الْقَرْيَةِ وَخَيْرَ
أَهْلِهَا، وَخَيْرَ مَا فِيهَا، وَأَعُوذُ بِكَ مِنْ شَرِّهَا، وَشَرِّ
أَهْلِهَا، وَشَرِّ مَا فِيهَا».

Allaahumma Rabbas-samaawaatis sab'i wa maa 'adhlalna, wa Rabbal 'aradheenas-sab'i wa maa 'aqlalna, wa Rabbash-shayaateeni wa maa 'adhlalna, wa Rabbar-riyaahi wa maa tharayna. 'As'aluka khayra haathi-hil-qaryati wa khayra 'ahlihaa, wa khayra maafeehaa, wa 'a'oothu bika min sharrihaa, wa sharri 'ahlihaa, wa sharri maa feehaa.

O Allāh, Lord of the seven heavens and all they overshadow, Lord of the seven worlds and all they uphold, Lord of the devils and all they lead astray, Lord of the winds and all they scatter. I ask You for the goodness of this town and for the goodness of its people, and for the goodness it contains. I seek refuge in You from its evil, from the evil of its people and from the evil it contains.[250]

---

98. When entering a market

٢٠٩-«لَا إِلٰهَ إِلَّا اللهُ وَحْدَهُ لَا شَرِيكَ لَهُ، لَهُ الْمُلْكُ وَلَهُ الْحَمْدُ يُحْيِي وَيُمِيتُ وَهُوَ حَيٌّ لَا يَمُوتُ، بِيَدِهِ الْخَيْرُ، وَهُوَ عَلَى كُلِّ شَيْءٍ قَدِيرٌ».

Laa 'ilaaha 'illallaahu wahdahu laa shareeka lahu, lahul-mulku wa lahul-hamdu, yuhyee wa yumeetu, wa Huwa hayyun laa yamootu, biyadihil-khayru, wa Huwa 'alaa kulli shay'in Qadeer.

None has the right to be worshipped but Allāh alone, Who has no partner. His is the

---

250. Al-Hākim who graded it authentic and Ath-Thahabi agreed 2/100, and Ibn As-Sunni (no. 524). Al-Hāfidh; graded it good in his checking of Al-'Athkār 5/154. Ibn Bāz said in *Tuhfatul 'Akhyār* p. 37, that An-Nasā'i recorded it with a good chain of narration.

dominion and His is the praise. He brings life and He causes death, and He is living and does not die. In His Hand is all good, and He is Able to do all things.[251]

◆

99. When your vehicle or mount fails

٢١٠-«بِسْمِ اللهِ».

210. *Bismillaahi.* With the Name of Allāh.[252]

◆

100. For the traveler who leaves someone behind

٢١١-«أَسْتَوْدِعُكُمُ اللهَ الَّذِي لَا تَضِيعُ وَدَائِعُهُ».

'Astawdi 'ukumul-laahal-lathee laa tadhee'u wadaa'i'uhu.

---

251. At-Tirmithi 5/291, and Al-Hākim 1/538. Al-Albāni graded it good in *Sahīh Ibn Mājah* 2/21 and *Sahīh At-Tirmithi* 3/152.

252. Abu Dawud 4/296. Al-Albāni graded it authentic in *Sahīh Abu Dawud* 3/941.

I leave you in the care of Allāh, as nothing is lost that is in His care.[253]

- - - - - - - - ◆ - - - - - - - -

101. By the resident for the traveler

٢١٢-«أَسْتَوْدِعُ اللهَ دِينَكَ، وَأَمَانَتَكَ، وَخَوَاتِيمَ عَمَلِكَ».

'Astawdi'ullaaha deenaka, wa 'amaanataka, wa khawaateema 'amalika.

I leave your religion in the care of Allāh, as well as your safety, and the last of your deeds.[254]

- - - - - - - - ◆ - - - - - - - -

٢١٣-«زَوَّدَكَ اللهُ التَّقْوَى، وَغَفَرَ ذَنْبَكَ، وَيَسَّرَ لَكَ الْخَيْرَ حَيْثُ مَا كُنْتَ».

Zawwadakal-laahut-taqwaa, wa ghafara thanbaka, wa yassara lakal-khayra haythu maa kunta.

---

253. Aḥmad 2/403, Ibn Mājah 2/943. See also Al-Albāni, *Saḥīḥ Ibn Mājah* 2/133.

254. Aḥmad 2/7, At-Tirmithi 5/499. See also Al-Albāni, *Saḥīḥ At-Tirmithi* 2/155.

May Allāh give you piety as your provision, forgive your sins, and make goodness easy for you wherever you are.[255]

◆

102. For glorifying Allāh on the journey

Jabir ﷺ said: Whenever we went up a hill we would say *Allaahu 'Akbar* (Allāh is the Most Great) and when we descended we would say *Subhaanallaah* (Glory is to Allāh).[256]

◆

103. For traveler at dawn

٢١٥-«سَمِعَ سَامِعٌ بِحَمْدِ اللهِ، وَحُسْنِ بَلَائِهِ عَلَيْنَا. رَبَّنَا صَاحِبْنَا، وَأَفْضِلْ عَلَيْنَا عَائِذًا بِاللهِ مِنَ النَّارِ».

Sami'a saami'un bihamdillaahi wa husni balaa'ihi 'alaynaa. Rabbanaa saahibnaa, wa 'afdhil 'alaynaa 'aa'ithan billaahi minan-naar.

---

255. At-Tirmithi. See Al-Albāni, *Sahīh At-Tirmithi* 3/155.
256. Al-Bukhāri, cf. Al-Asqalāni, *Fathul-Bāri* 6/135.

He Who listens has heard that we praise Allāh for the good things He gives us. Our Lord, be with us and bestow Your favour upon us. I seek the protection of Allāh from the Fire.[257]

---

104. When stopping over on the journey

٢١٦-«أَعُوذُ بِكَلِمَاتِ اللهِ التَّامَّاتِ مِنْ شَرِّ مَا خَلَقَ».

'A'oo<u>th</u>u bikalimaatil-laahit-taammaati min sharri maa <u>kh</u>alaq.

---

257. Muslim 4/2086, the meaning of *sami'a saami'un* (who listens has heard) is that 'a witness has witnessed our praise of Allāh due to His blessings and favor upon us.' It could also be read *samma'a saami'un*, in which case it means 'one who has heard this statement of mine will convey it to another and he will say it as well.' This is due to the attention given to the *Thikr* (remembrance of Allāh) and supplications made during the early morning hours. The meaning of his saying 'Our Lord, be with us and bestow Your favor upon us' is: 'Our Lord, protect us and guard us. Bless us with Your numerous bounties, and avert from us every evil.' See An-Nawawi, *Sharh Sahīh Muslim* 17/39.

I seek refuge in the Perfect Words of Allāh from the evil of what He has created.[258]

---◆---

105. Upon returning from a journey

From every elevated point say Allaahu 'Akbar (Allāh is the Most Great) three times and then recite:

٢١٧-«لَا إِلَهَ إِلَّا اللهُ وَحْدَهُ لَا شَرِيكَ لَهُ، لَهُ الْمُلْكُ وَلَهُ الْحَمْدُ، وَهُوَ عَلَى كُلِّ شَيْءٍ قَدِيرٌ، آيِبُونَ، تَائِبُونَ، عَابِدُونَ، لِرَبِّنَا حَامِدُونَ، صَدَقَ اللهُ وَعْدَهُ، وَنَصَرَ عَبْدَهُ، وَهَزَمَ الْأَحْزَابَ وَحْدَهُ».

Laa 'ilaaha 'illallaahu wahdahu laa sharee-ka lahu, lahul-mulku, wa lahul hamdu, wa Huwa 'alaa kulli shay'in Qadeer, 'aa'iboona, taa'iboona, 'aabidoona, lirabbinaa haami-doona, sadaqallaahu wa'dahu, wa nasara 'abdahu, wa hazamal 'ahzaaba wahdahu.

---

258. Muslim 4/2080.

None has the right to be worshipped but Allāh alone, Who has no partner. His is the dominion and His is the praise, and He is Able to do all things. We return repentant to our Lord, worshipping our Lord, and praising our Lord. He fulfilled His Promise, He aided His slave, and He alone defeated the Confederates.[259]

---

106. When something pleasing or displeasing happens

When something happened that pleased him, the Prophet ﷺ used to say:

٢١٨-«الْحَمْدُ لله الَّذِي بِنِعْمَتِهِ تَتِمُّ الصَّالِحَاتُ».

Alhamdu lillaahil-lathee bini'matihi tatimmus-saalihaat.

Praise is to Allāh Who by His blessings all good things are perfected.

---

259. Bukhari 7/163, Muslim 2/980. The Prophet ﷺ used to say this on returning from a campaign or from *Hajj*.

And if something happened that displeased him, he used to say:

«الْحَمْدُ لله عَلَى كُلِّ حَالٍ».

Alhamdu lillaahi 'alaa kulli haal.

Praise is to Allāh in all circumstances.[260]

---

107. The excellence of asking for Allāh's blessings upon the Prophet ﷺ

The Prophet ﷺ said: "Whoever prays for Allāh's blessings upon me once, will be blessed for it by Allāh ten times." [261]

The Prophet ﷺ said: "Do not make my grave a place of ritual celebration, but pray

---

260. Ibn As-Sunni, *'Amalul-Yawm wal-Laylah*, and Al-Ḥākim who graded it authentic 1/499. See also Al-Albāni, *Saḥīhul-Jami' As-Saghir* 4/201.
261. Muslim 1/288.

for Allāh's blessings upon me, for your blessings reach me from wherever you are."[262]

The Prophet ﷺ said: "The miser is the one in whose presence I am mentioned yet does not pray for Allāh's blessings upon me."[263]

The Prophet ﷺ said: "Indeed Allāh has angels who roam the earth and they convey to me the greetings (or prayers of peace) of my 'Ummah (nation)."[264]

The Prophet ﷺ said: "No one sends greetings (or prayers of peace) upon me but Allāh returns my soul to me so that I may return his greetings."[265]

---

262. Abu Dawud 2/218, Aḥmad 2/367. Al-Albāni graded it authentic in *Sahīh Abu Dawud* 2/383.

263. At-Tirmithi 5/551 and others. See also Al-Albāni, *Sahīh At-Tirmithi* 3/177 and *Sahīhul Jāmi' As-Saghir* 3/25.

264. An-Nasā'i, Al-Hākim 2/421. Al-Albāni graded it authentic in *Sahīh An-Nasā'i* 1/274.

265. Abu Dawud (no. 2041). Al-Albāni graded it good in *Sahīh AbuDawud* 1/383.

108. For spreading *Salâm* (the greetings of peace)

The Prophet ﷺ said: "You shall not enter Paradise until you believe, and you have not believed until you love one another. Shall I tell you of something you can do to make you love one another?

Spread the greetings of *Salâm* (peace) amongst yourselves (i.e. between each other)."[266]

The Prophet ﷺ said: "There are three things which whoever gathers all of them together, then he has gathered *Imān* (Faith): justice with oneself, greeting people with greetings of *Salām* (peace), and freeing oneself from stinginess."[267]

Abdullah bin 'Umar ﷺ said: A man asked the Prophet ﷺ, "What is the best act of Islam?"

---

266. Muslim 1/74 and others.
267. Al-Bukhāri, cf. Al-Asqalāni, *Fathul-Bāri* 1/82 as a statement of the Companion 'Ammar ﷺ.

He ﷺ said, "To feed others and to give greetings of *Salām* (peace) to those whom you know and to those whom you do not know."[268]

---

109. Replying to a disbeliever's *Salām*

If people of the Scriptures (i.e. Christians and Jews) greet you with *As Salaamu 'alaykum*, then say (to them):

«وَعَلَيْكُمْ».

Wa 'alaykum.[269] And upon you.

---

268. Al-Bukhāri, cf. Al-Asqalāni, *Fathul-Bāri* 1/55, Muslim 1/65.

269. Al-Bukhāri, cf. Al-Asqalāni, *Fathul-Bāri* 11/42, Muslim 4/1705.

110. On hearing the cock's crow or a donkey's braying

When you hear the cock's crow, ask Allāh for His favour upon you for surely it has seen an angel. When you hear the bray of a donkey, seek refuge in Allāh from Satan, for surely it has seen a devil.[270]

---◆---

111. On hearing a dog barking in the night

When you hear a dog barking or a donkey braying in the night, then seek refuge in Allāh from them, for surely they have seen what you see not.[271]

---◆---

---

270. Al-Bukhāri, cf. Al-Asqalāni, *Fathul-Bāri* 6/350, Muslim 4/2092.
271. Abu Dawud 4/327, Aḥmad 3/306. Al-Albāni graded it authentic in *Sahīh Abu Dawud* 3/961.

112. For someone you have spoken ill about

٢٣٠- «اللَّهُمَّ فَأَيُّمَا مُؤْمِنٍ سَبَبْتُهُ فَاجْعَلْ ذَلِكَ لَهُ قُرْبَةً إِلَيْكَ يَوْمَ الْقِيَامَةِ»

Allaahumma fa'ayyumaa mu'minin sababtuhu faj'al thaalika lahu qurbatan 'ilayka yawmal-qiyaamati

O Allāh, whomever of the believers I have abused, give him the reward of a sacrificial slaughter for it on the Day of Resurrection.[272]

---

113. How a Muslim should praise another Muslim

If any of you praises his companion then let him say:

«أَحْسِبُ فُلَانًا وَاللهُ حَسِيبُهُ».

---

272. Al-Bukhāri, cf. Al-Asqalāni, *Fathul-Bāri* 11/171, Muslim 4/2007. The wording in Muslim's report is: 'make it a purification for him and a source of mercy.'

'Ahsibu fulaanan wallaahu haseebuhu.

I consider (such and such a person), and Allāh is his Assessor.

«وَلَا أُزَكِّي عَلَى اللهِ أَحَدًا».

Wa laa 'uzakkee 'alallaahi 'ahadan.

(meaning: and I cannot claim anyone to be pious before Allāh) if you know of this (good character trait in the person) to be such and such (saying what he thinks is praiseworthy in that person).[273]

◆

114. When you are praised

٢٣٢-«اللّٰهُمَّ لَا تُؤَاخِذْنِي بِمَا يَقُولُونَ، وَاغْفِرْ لِي مَا لَا يَعْلَمُونَ [وَاجْعَلْنِي خَيْرًا مِمَّا يَظُنُّونَ]».

Allaahumma laa tu'aakhithnee bimaa

---

273. Muslim 4 /2296.

yaqooloona, waghfir lee maa laa ya'lamoona [waj'alnee khayram-mimmaa yadhunnoon].

O Allāh, do not call me to account for what they say and forgive me for what they have no knowledge of [and make me better than they imagine].[274]

---------------- • ----------------

115. The pilgrim's announcement upon his arrival for *Hajj* or *'Umrah*

٢٣٣ –«لَبَّيْكَ اللَّهُمَّ لَبَّيْكَ، لَبَّيْكَ لَا شَرِيكَ لَكَ لَبَّيْكَ، إِنَّ الْحَمْدَ، وَالنِّعْمَةَ، لَكَ وَالْمُلْكَ، لَا شَرِيكَ لَكَ».

Labbayk Allaahumma labbayk, labbayk laa shareeka laka labbayk, 'innal hamda, wan-ni'mata, laka walmulk, laa shareeka laka.

I am here at Your service, O Allāh, I am here at Your service. I am here at Your service,

---

274. Al-Bukhāri, *Al-'Adabul-Mufrad* no. 761. See Al-Albāni, *Sahīh Al-'Adabul-Mufrad* (no. 585). The portion between brackets is from Al-Bayhaqi, *Shu'ab Al-Imān* 4/228, and comes another account.

You have no partner, I am here at Your service. Surely the praise, and blessings are Yours, and the dominion. You have no partner.[275]

116. When passing in front of the Black Stone during *Tawâf*

The Prophet ﷺ performed *Tawâf* riding a camel. Every time he passed the corner of the *Kāba* containing the Black Stone, he would point to it with something that he was holding and say: *Allaahu 'Akbar* (Allāh is the Most Great!)[276]

---

275. Al-Bukhāri, cf. Al-Asqalāni, *Fathul-Bāri* 3/408, Muslim 2/841.

276. Al-Bukhāri, cf. Al-Asqalāni, *Fathul-Bāri* 3/476. See also 472. The 'something' that was referred to in this *Hadith* was a cane.

117. To recite between the Yemenite Corner and the Black Stone

٢٣٥- ﴿رَبَّنَا ءَاتِنَا فِي ٱلدُّنْيَا حَسَنَةً وَفِي ٱلْأَخِرَةِ حَسَنَةً وَقِنَا عَذَابَ ٱلنَّارِ﴾

Rabbanaa 'aatinaa fid-dunyaa Hasanatan wa fil-'aakhirati Hasanatan wa qinaa 'athaaban-naar.

Our Lord, grant us the good things in this world and the good things in the next life and save us from the punishment of the Fire.[277]

---◆---

118. To recite standing at Safa and Marwah

Whenever the Prophet ﷺ approached Mount Safa, he would recite:

---

277. Abu Dawud 2/179, Aḥmad 3/411, Al-Baghawi, *Sharhus-Sunnah* 7/128. Al-Albāni graded it good in *Sahīh Abu Dawud* 1/354. The *'Āyat* is from *Surat Al-Baqarah*, 2:201.

«﴿إِنَّ ٱلصَّفَا وَٱلْمَرْوَةَ مِن شَعَآئِرِ ٱللَّهِ﴾ أَبْدَأُ بِمَا بَدَأَ اللهُ بِهِ».

’Innas-Safaa wal-Marwata min sha‘aa’iril-laah. ’Abda’u bimaa bada’allaahu bihi.

Surely Safa and Marwah are among the signs of Allāh. I begin by that which Allāh began.

He ﷺ began (his *Sa‘y*) at Mount Safa climbing it until he could see the House. He then faced the *Qiblah* repeating the words:

Laa ’ilaaha ’illallaah, Allaahu ’Akbar.

«لَا إِلَهَ إِلَّا اللهُ، اللهُ أَكْبَرُ».

There is none worthy of worship but Allāh, and Allāh is the Most Great.

Then he ﷺ said:

«لَا إِلَهَ إِلَّا اللهُ وَحْدَهُ لَا شَرِيكَ لَهُ، لَهُ الْمُلْكُ وَلَهُ الْحَمْدُ، وَهُوَ عَلَى كُلِّ شَيْءٍ قَدِيرٌ، لَا إِلَهَ إِلَّا اللهُ وَحْدَهُ، أَنْجَزَ وَعْدَهُ، وَنَصَرَ عَبْدَهُ، وَهَزَمَ الْأَحْزَابَ وَحْدَهُ».

Laa 'ilaaha 'illallaahu wahdahu laa shareeka lahu, lahul-mulku wa lahul-hamdu wa Huwa 'alaa kulli shay'in Qadeer, laa 'ilaaha 'illallaahu wahdahu, 'anjaza wa'dahu, wa nasara 'abdahu, wa hazamal 'ahzaaba wahdahu.

None has the right to be worshipped but Allāh alone, Who has no partner, His is the dominion and His is the praise, and He is Able to do all things. None has the right to be worshipped but Allāh alone, He fulfilled His Promise, He aided His slave, and He alone defeated Confederates.

Then he would ask Allāh for what he liked. He would repeat this three times. He would do the same at Mount Marwah as he did at Mount Safa.[278]

-------------- ◆ --------------

278. Muslim 2/888.

119. On the Day of Arafât

The Prophet ﷺ said: The best invocation is that of the Day of Arafât, and the best that anyone can say is what I and the Prophets before me have said:

٢٣٧-«لَا إِلَهَ إِلَّا اللهُ وَحْدَهُ لَا شَرِيكَ لَهُ، لَهُ الْمُلْكُ وَلَهُ الْحَمْدُ، وَهُوَ عَلَى كُلِّ شَيْءٍ قَدِيرٌ».

Laa 'ilaaha 'illallaahu wahdahu laa shareeka lahu, lahul-mulku wa lahul-hamdu wa Huwa 'alaa kulli shay'in Qadeer.

None has the right to be worshipped but Allāh alone, Who has no partner. His is the dominion and His is the praise, and He is Able to do all things.[279]

--------------- ◆ ---------------

---

279. At-Tirmithi. Al-Albāni graded it good in *Sahīh At-Tirmithi* 3/184, and also *Silsilatul-'Ahādīth As Sahīhah* 4/6.

120. At the sacred Muzdalifah

The Prophet☺ rode his camel, *Al Qaswa'*, until he reached the sacred area (*Al-Mash'ar-il-Haraam*). Then he faced the *Qiblah* and invoked Allāh, and repeatedly said the words: *Allaahu 'Akbar* (Allāh is the Most Great), *Allaahu 'Ahad* (Allāh is One) and *Laa 'ilaaha 'illallaah* (There is none worthy of worship but Allāh). He remained stationary until the sky became yellow with the dawn, and then pressed on before sunrise.[280]

---------- ◆ ----------

121. While stoning the three pillars at Mina

The Prophet ☺ said *Allaahu 'Akbar* (Allāh is the Most Great) with each pebble he threw at the three pillars. Then he went forward, stood facing the *Qiblah* and raised his hands and called upon Allāh. That was after (stoning) the first and second pillar. As for the third, he stoned it and called out *Allaahu 'Akbar* with

---

280. Muslim 2/891.

every pebble he threw, but when he finished he left without standing at it (for supplications).[281]

◆

122. When you are surprised or startled

٢٤٠ - «سُبْحَانَ اللهِ».

Subhaanallaah! (Glory is to Allāh).[282]

٢٤١ - «اللهُ أَكْبَرُ».

Allaahu 'Akbar! (Allāh is the Most Great)[283]

◆

---

281. Al-Bukhari, cf. Al-Asqalani, *Fathul-Bāri* 3/581, 3, 4, and Muslim

282. Al-Bukhari, cf. Al-Asqalani, *Fathul-Bāri* 1/210, 390, 414 and Muslim 4/1857.

283. Al-Bukhari, cf. Al-Asqalani, *Fathul-Bāri* 8/441. See also Al-Albāni, *Sahīh At-Tirmithi* 2/103, 235, Aḥmad 5/218.

123. When something pleases you

Whenever something happened that pleased him or made him happy, the Prophet ﷺ used to prostrate himself in thanks to Allāh, the Blessed, the All-Mighty.[284]

------------------ ◆ ------------------

124. When you feel a pain in your body

Put your hand on the place where you feel pain and say (three times):

«بِسْمِ اللهِ» .

Bismillaah. With the Name of Allāh.

Then say:

«أَعُوذُ بِاللهِ وَقُدْرَتِهِ مِنْ شَرِّ مَا أَجِدُ وَأُحَاذِرُ» .

'A'oothu billaahi wa qudratihi min sharri maa 'ajidu wa 'uhaathiru.

------

284. Abu Dawud, Ibn Mājah, At-Tirmithi. See also Al-Albāni, *Sahīh Ibn Mājah* 1/233, and *'Irwa'ul-Ghalīl* 2/226.

I seek refuge in Allāh and in His Power from the evil of what I find and of what I guard against.[285]

---

125. When you fear you may afflict someone with the evil eye

If you see anything of your brother that pleases you, or of his person or of his property [then ask Allāh to bless him in it] for the envious eye is real.[286]

---

126. When you feel frightened

«٢٤٥–"لَا إِلَهَ إِلَّا الله".»

245. *Laa 'ilaaha 'illallaah!*

---

285. Muslim 4/1728.

286. Aḥmad 4/447, Ibn Mājāh, Malik. Al-Albāni graded it authentic in *Sahīhul-Jami' As-Saghir* 1/212. Also see Al-Arna'ut's checking of Ibn Al-Qayyim's *Zādul-Ma'ād* 4/170.

There is none worthy of worship but Allāh![287]

--------------- ◆ ---------------

127. When slaughtering or sacrificing an animal

٢٤٦ –«بِسْمِ اللهِ وَاللهُ أَكْبَرُ [اللَّهُمَّ مِنْكَ وَلَكَ] اللَّهُمَّ تَقَبَّلْ مِنِّي».

Bismillaahi wallaahu 'Akbar [Allaahumma minka wa laka] Allaahumma taqabbal minnee.

With the Name of Allāh, Allāh is the Most Great! (O Allāh, from You and to You.] O Allāh, accept it from me.[288]

--------------- ◆ ---------------

128. To foil the devil's plots

٢٤٧ –أَعُوذُ بِكَلِمَاتِ اللهِ التَّامَّاتِ الَّتِي لَا يُجَاوِزُهُنَّ بَرٌّ
وَلَا فَاجِرٌ مِنْ شَرِّ مَا خَلَقَ، وَبَرَأَ وَذَرَأَ، وَمِنْ شَرِّ مَا يَنْزِلُ

---

287. Al-Bukhāri, cf. Al-Asqalāni, *Fathul-Bāri* 6/181, Muslim 4/2208.
288. Muslim 3/1557, Al-Bayhaqi 9/287.

مِنَ السَّمَاءِ، وَمِنْ شَرِّ مَا يَعْرُجُ فِيهَا، وَمِنْ شَرِّ مَا ذَرَأَ فِي
الْأَرْضِ، وَمِنْ شَرِّ مَا يَخْرُجُ مِنْهَا، وَمِنْ شَرِّ فِتَنِ اللَّيْلِ
وَالنَّهَارِ، وَمِنْ شَرِّ كُلِّ طَارِقٍ إِلَّا طَارِقًا يَطْرُقُ بِخَيْرٍ يَا
رَحْمٰنُ».

'A'oothu bikalimaatil-laahit-taammaatil-
-latee laa yujaawizuhunna barrun wa laa
faajirun min sharri maa khalaqa, wa bara'a
wa thara'a, wa min sharri maa yanzilu
minas-samaa'i, wa min sharri maa ya'ruju
feehaa, wa min sharri maa thara'a fil-'ard-
hi, wa min sharri ma yakhruju minhaa, wa
min sharri fitanil-layli wannahaari, wa min
sharri kulli taariqin 'illaa taariqan yatruqu
bikhayrin yaa Rahmaan.

I seek refuge in the Perfect Words of Allāh
– which neither the upright nor the corrupt
may overcome – from the evil of what He
created, of what He made, and of what He
scattered, from the evil of what descends
from the heavens, and of what rises up to
them, from the evil of what He scattered in
the earth and of what emerges from it, from

the evil trials of night and day, and from the evil of every night visitor, except the night visitor who comes with good. O Merciful One.[289]

---------- • ----------

129. For repentance and seeking forgiveness

Allāh's Messenger ﷺ said: "By Allāh, I seek the forgiveness of Allāh, and repent to Him more than seventy times in a day."[290]

Allāh's Messenger ﷺ said: "O people, repent to Allāh, for I verily repent to Him one hundred times a day."[291]

Allāh 's Messenger ﷺ said: Whoever says:

«أَسْتَغْفِرُاللهَ الْعَظِيمَ الَّذِي لَا إِلَهَ إِلَّا هُوَ الْحَيُّ الْقَيُّومُ وَأَتُوبُ إِلَيْهِ»

---

289. Aḥmad 3/419, with an authentic chain of narration, and Ibn As-Sunni (no. 637). Al Arna'ut, graded its chain authentic in his checking of *Al-'Aqīdah At-Tahawīyyah* p.133. See also *Majma'uz-Zawā'id*, 10/127.

290. Al-Bukhari, cf. Al-Asqalāni, *Fathul-Bāri* 11/101.

291. Muslim 4/2076.

'Astaghfirullaahal-'A<u>dh</u>eemal-la<u>th</u>ee laa
'ilaaha 'illaa Huwal-Hayyul-Qayyoomu wa
'atoobu 'ilayhi.

I seek the forgiveness of Allāh the Mighty,
Whom there is none worthy of worship except Him, the Living, the Eternal, and I repent
to Him, Allāh will forgive him even if he has
deserted the army's ranks.[292]

Allāh's Messenger ﷺ said: "The closest that
the Lord comes to the slave is in the last
portion of the night. So, if you are able to
be among those who remember Allāh in this
hour, then be among them.[293]

Allāh's Messenger ﷺ said: "The closest that
the slave comes to his Lord is when he is

---

292. Abu Dawud 2/85, At-Tirmi<u>th</u>i 5/569, and Al-Hākim
who declared it authentic and A<u>th</u>-<u>Th</u>ahabi agreed
with him 1/511. Al-Albāni graded it authentic in
Sahīh At-Tirmi<u>th</u>i 3/182. See also Jāmi'ul-'Usool li-
'Ahādith Ar-Rasool 4/389-90 checked by Al-Arna'ut.

293. At-Tirmi<u>th</u>i, An-Nasā'i 1/279 andAl-Hākim. See also
Al-Albāni, Sahīh At-Tirmi<u>th</u>i 3/183, and Jāmi'ul-
'Usool with Al-Arna'ut's checking 4/144.

prostrating, so invoke Allāh much (in prostration)."[294]

Allāh's Messenger ﷺ said: "It is a heavy thing for my heart if I do not seek Allāh's forgiveness a hundred times a day."[295]

◆

130. The excellence of remembering Allāh

Allāh's Messenger ﷺ said: Whoever says:

«سُبْحَانَ اللهِ وَبِحَمْدِهِ».

Subhaanallaahi wa bihamdihi.

Glorified is Allāh and praised is He –

---

294. Muslim 1/350.

295. Muslim 4/2075. Ibn 'Athīr explains that the Prophet ﷺ was always vigilant in his remembrance and drawing near to Allāh, and if he forgot to do any of what he normally did from time to time, or it slipped his mind, he felt as if he had wronged himself and so he would begin to seek the forgiveness of Allāh. See *Jāmi'ul-'Usool* 4/386.

one hundred times a day, will have his sins forgiven even if they are like the foam of the sea.[296]

◆

Allāh's Messenger ﷺ said: Whoever says the following, ten times, will have the reward for freeing four slaves from the Children of Isma'il.[297]

«لَا إِلَهَ إِلَّا اللهُ وَحْدَهُ لَا شَرِيكَ لَهُ، لَهُ الْمُلْكُ وَلَهُ الْحَمْدُ، وَهُوَ عَلَى كُلِّ شَيْءٍ قَدِيرٌ».

Laa 'ilaaha 'illallaahu wahdahu laa sharee-ka lahu, lahul-mulku wa lahul-hamdu wa Huwa 'alaa kullishay'in Qadeer.

None has the right to be worshipped but Allāh alone Who has no partner. His is the dominion and His is the praise, and He is Able to do all things.

---

296. Al-Bukhāri 7/168, Muslim 4/2071, see also invocation no. 91 of this book.

297. Al-Bukhāri 7/67, Muslim 4/2071, see also invocation no. 93 of this book.

Allāh's Messenger ﷺ said: Two words are light on the tongue but weigh heavily in the balance, and are loved by the Most Merciful One:

«سُبْحَانَ اللهِ وَبِحَمْدِهِ سُبْحَانَ اللهِ الْعَظِيمِ».

Subhaanal-laahi wa bihamdihi, Subhaanal-laahil-'Adheem.

Glorified is Allāh and praised is He, Glorified is Allāh the Most Great.[298]

──────────── • ────────────

Allāh's Messenger ﷺ said: For me to say –

«سُبْحَانَ اللهِ، وَالْحَمْدُ للهِ، وَلَا إِلَهَ إِلَّا اللهُ، وَاللهُ أَكْبَرُ».

Subhaanallaahi, walhamdu lillaahi, wa laa 'ilaaha 'illallaahu, wallaahu 'Akbar.

Glory is to Allāh, and praise is to Allāh, and there is none worthy of worship but Allāh,

────────────────────

298. Al-Bukhāri 7/168, Muslim 4/2072.

and Allāh is the Most Great – is dearer to me than all that the sun rises upon (i.e. the whole world).[299]

Allāh's Messenger ﷺ said, "Is anyone of you incapable of earning one thousand *Hasanah* (rewards) in a day?" Someone from his gathering asked, "How can anyone of us earn a thousand *Hasanah*?" He said, "Glorify Allāh a hundred times and a thousand *Hasanah* will be written for you, or a thousand sins will be wiped away."[300]

Whoever says:

«سُبْحَانَ اللهِ الْعَظِيمِ وَبِحَمْدِهِ».

Subhaanallaahil-'A<u>dh</u>eemi wa bihamdihi.

Glorified is Allāh the Most Great and praised

---

299. Muslim 4/2072.
300. Muslim 4/2073.

is He – will have a date palm planted for him in Paradise.[301]

---◆---

Allāh's Messenger ﷺ said, "O Abdullah bin Qais, should I not point you to one of the treasures of Paradise?" He said, "Yes, O Messenger of Allāh." So he told me to say:

«لَا حَوْلَ وَلَا قُوَّةَ إِلَّا بِاللهِ».

Laa hawla wa laa quwwata 'illaa billaah.

There is no power and no might except by Allāh.[302]

---◆---

---

301. At-Tirmithi 5/511, and Al-Hākim who graded it authentic and Ath-Thahabi agreed 1/501. See also Al-Albāni, *Sahīhul-Jami' As-Saghir* 5/531 and *Sahīh At-Tirmithi* 3/160.

302. Al-Bukhāri, cf. Al-Asqalāni, *Fathul-Bāri* 11/213, Muslim 4/2076.

Allāh's Messenger ﷺ said: The most beloved words to Allāh are four:

«سُبْحَانَ الله».

Subhaanallaah. Glorified is Allāh;

«وَالْحَمْدُ لله».

Walhamdu lillaah. The praise is for Allāh;

«وَلَا إِلَهَ إِلَّا الله».

Wa laa 'ilaaha 'illallaah. There is none worthy of worship but Allāh; and

«وَالله أَكْبَرُ».

Wallaahu 'Akbar. Allāh is the Most Great.

It does not matter which one you start by.[303]

---

303. Muslim 3/1685.

A desert Arab came to Allāh's Messenger ﷺ
and said, "Teach me a word that I can say."
The Prophet ﷺ told him to say:

«لَا إِلَهَ إِلَّا اللهُ وَحْدَهُ لَا شَرِيكَ لَهُ، اللهُ أَكْبَرُ كَبِيرًا،
وَالْحَمْدُ للهِ كَثِيرًا، سُبْحَانَ اللهِ رَبِّ الْعَالَمِينَ، لَا حَوْلَ
وَلَا قُوَّةَ إِلَّا بِاللهِ الْعَزِيزِ الْحَكِيمِ».

*Laa 'ilaaha 'illallaahu wahdahu laa shareeka
lahu, Allaahu 'Akbaru kabeeran, walhamdu
lillaahi katheeran, Subhaanallaahi Rabbil
'aalameen, laa hawla wa laa quwwata 'illaa
billaahil-'Azeezil-Hakeem.*

There is none worthy of worship but Allāh,
Who has no partner, Allāh is the Great, the
Most Great, and praise is to Allāh in abun-
dance, glory is to Allāh, Lord of the worlds.
There is no power and no might but by Allāh
the Mighty, the Wise.

He said, "That is for my Lord, but what
about me?" The Prophet ﷺ told him to say:

«اللَّهُمَّ اغْفِرْ لِي، وَارْحَمْنِي، وَاهْدِنِي وَارْزُقْنِي» .

Allaahummaghfir lee, warhamnee, wahdinee warzuqnee.

O Allāh forgive me, and have mercy on me, and guide me, and provide for me.[304]

Whenever anyone accepted Islam, the Prophet ﷺ used to teach him how to pray, then he would instruct him to invoke Allāh with the following words:

«اللَّهُمَّ اغْفِرْ لِي، وَارْحَمْنِي، وَاهْدِنِي، وَعَافِنِي وَارْزُقْنِي» .

Allaahummaghfir lee, warhamnee, wahdinee, wa 'aafinee warzuqnee.

---

304. Muslim 4/2072, Abu Dawud reports the same *Hadith* with the addition: and when the Arab left, the Prophet ﷺ said: "He has filled his hands with goodness." 1/220.

O Allāh forgive me, and have mercy on me, and guide me, and give me good health and provide for me.[305]

The most excellent invocation is:

«الْحَمْدُ لِلَّهِ».

Alhamdu lillaah. Praise is for Allāh.

And the most excellent words of remembrance are:

«لَا إِلَهَ إِلَّا اللَّهُ».

Laa 'ilaaha 'illallaah. There is none worthy of worship but Allāh.[306]

---

305. Muslim 4/2073, and in one of Muslim's reports there is the addition: 'For these words combine (the goodness of) this world and the next.'

306. At-Tirmithi 5/462, Ibn Mājah 2/1249, and Al-Hākim who graded it authentic and Ath-Thahabi agreed 1/503. See Al-Albāni, *Sahīhul-Jāmi' As-Saghir* 1/362.

The good deeds which endure are :

«سُبْحَانَ اللهِ» .

Subhaanallaah. Glorified is Allāh; and

«وَالْحَمْدُ للهِ» .

Walhamdu lillaah. The praise is for Allāh; and

«وَلَا إِلَهَ إِلَّا اللهُ» .

Wa laa 'ilaaha 'illallaah. There is none worthy of worship but Allāh; and

«وَاللهُ أَكْبَرُ» .

Wallaahu 'Akbar. Allāh is the Most Great; and

«وَلَا حَوْلَ وَلَا قُوَّةَ إِلَّا بِاللهِ»

Wa laa hawla wa laa quwwata 'illaa billaah.

There is no power and no might except by Allah.[307]

◆

131. How the Prophet ﷺ glorified Allāh

Abdullah bin 'Amr ﷺ said: "I saw the Prophet ﷺ counting the glorification of his Lord on his right hand."[308]

◆

132. Goodness and good etiquettes for community life

When evening descends, bring your children indoors for the devils scatter out at this hour. After the passing of the first hour of the night,

---

307. Aḥmad (no. 513) (Aḥmad Shakir, ed.) and its chain of narration is authentic. See *Majma'uz Zawā'id* 1/297. Ibn Hajar mentions it in *Bulughul-Marām* saying that Ibn Hibbān and Al-Hākim considered it authentic.

308. Abu Dawud with a different wording 2/81, and At-Tirmithi 5/521. See also Al-Albāni, *Sahīhul Jami' As-Saghir* 4/271 (no. 4865).

you may let the children go. Close your doors while mentioning the Name of Allāh, for the devil may not open a closed door. Fasten your waterskins mentioning the Name of Allāh. Cover your eating vessels mentioning the Name of Allāh even if you just put something over it, and extinguish your lamps.[309]

Peace and blessing be upon our Prophet, Muhammad, and upon his family and all his Companions.

309. Al-Bukhāri, cf. Al-Asqalāni, *Fathul-Bāri* 10/88, Muslim 3/1595.

Bibliography

Abu Dawud
  - *Sunan*

Aḥmad bin Hanbal (d. 241 H.)
  - *Al-Musnad*, 6 vols. Beirut: Al-Maktab
    Al-Islāmi.

Al-Albāni, Muhammad Nasir Ad-Dīn
  - *’Ahkamul-Janā’iz.*
  - *’Irwā’ul-Ghalīl.*
  - *Mukhtasar Shamā’il At-Tirmithi.*
  - *Sahīh Al-’Adab Al-Mufrad.*
  - *Sahīhul Jamī‘ As-Saghīr.*
  - *Sahīhut-Targhīb wat-Tarhīb.*
  - *Sahīh Sunan Ibn Mājah.*
  - *Sahīh Sunan At-Tirmithī*
  - *Silsilatul-’Ahādīth As-Sahīhah.*

Asqalāni Al-, see Ibn Hajar.

Baghawi, Abū Muhammad Al-Husain bin
Mas’ūd Al-Farrā’, Al-, (d. 516 H)
  - *Ma‘ālam At-Tanzīl* (*Tafsīr Al-Baghawi*),

in the margins of *Tafsīr Al-Khāzin*, 4 vols. Beirut: Dār Al-Fikr, 1979.

Bayhaqi, Abu Bakr Aḥmad bin Husain bin 'Ali, Al-, (d. 458 H)
- *As-Sunan Al-Kubra*, 10 vols. Beirut: Dār Al Fikr, n.d.
- *Shu'ab Al-Imān*.

Bukhāri, Abī 'Abdullāh Muhammad bin Ismā'il bin Ibrāhīm bin Al-Mughīrah bin Bardizbah Al Bukhāri Al-Ju'fi, Al-, (d.256 H.)
- *Sahīh Al-Bukhāri*, 8 vols. Istanbul: Maktabah Al-Islāmīyah, 1981.
- *Al-'Adab Al-Mufrad*

Haythami, Al-, *Majma 'uz-Zawā'id*.

Hakim, Al-Hāfidh Muhammad bin Abdullāh bin Muhammad, Al-,(d. 404 H)
- *Al-Mustadrak*, 4 vols. Beirut: Dār Al-Kitāb Al-'Arabī, n.d.

Ibn Al-'Athīr, see Shaibāni, Al-.

Ibn As-Sunnā
- *'Amalul-Yawm wal-Laylah*

Ibn Bāz, 'Abdul 'Aziz
  - *Tuhfatul-'Akhyār*

Ibn Hajar Al-'Asqalāni, Aḥmad bin 'Alī (d. 852 H)
  - *Fathul-Bāri: Sharh Sahīh Al-Bukhāri*, 13 vols. Beirut: Mustafā Al-Halabī, n.d.

Ibn Hibbān
  - *Mawārid*

Ibn Hibbān, Abī Hātim Muhammad bin Hibbān Al-Busti (d. 354 H)
  - *Sahīh Ibn Hibbān*, Beirut: Mu'assasah Al-Risālah, 1984.

Ibn Khuzaymah, Ibn Mājah
  - *Sahīh Sunan Ibn Mājah*, (ed. Muhammad Nasir Ad-Dīn Al-Albāni, Riyadh: 1408/1988).

Ibn Mājah, Al-Hāfidh Abī 'Abdullāh Muhammad bin Yazīd Al-Qazwīnī (d. 283 H)
  - *Sunan Ibn Mājah*, 4 vols. Riyadh: Sharikah Al-Tibā'ah Al-'Arabīyah Al-Sa'udiyah, 1404/ 1984.

Ibn Qayyim Al-Jawziyyah, Abī 'Abdullah Muhammad bin Abī Bakr (d. 751 H)
- *Al-Wabil As-Sayyib*
- *Zādul-Ma'ād* (Al-Arnout & Arnout, ed.)

Ibn Qudāmah, Muwaffaq Ad-Din Abī Muhammad 'Abdullāh bin Ahmad bin Muhammad (d. 630 H.)
- *Kitābul-Mughnī*, 15 vols. Hijr: Cairo, 1990.

Mālik bin Anas, Abī 'Abdullāh Mālik bin Anas bin Abī 'Aamir bin 'Amr Al-Asbahī (d. 179 H.)
- *Al-Muwatta'*.

Muslim, Abī Al-Husain Muslim bin Al-Haijaj Al-Qushayri An-Nisāburi (d. 261 H.)
- *Sahih Muslim*, 5 vols. Beirut: Dār Ihyā' At-Turāth Al-'Arabī, n.d.

Nasā'ī, Abī 'Abd Al-Rahman Ahmad bin Shu'ayb bin 'Ali bin Bahr, Al-, (d. 303 H.)
- *Sunan Al-Nasā'ī*, 8 vols. Beirut: Dār Al-Kitāb Al-'Arabī, n.d.

- *Sahih Sunan An-Nasā'ī*
- *'Amalal-Yawm wal-Laylah*

Nawawi, Abī Zakarīyyā Yahyā bin Sharaf bin
Mūrī bin Hasan bin Husain bin Jum'a bin
Hizām Al-Hizāmi Al-Haurāni Muhī Al-Dīn,
Al-, (d. 676 н.)
- *Kitābul-'Athkār*, Beirut: Dār Al-Fikr, n.d.

Shaybāni, Ibn Al-'Athīr Al-Muhaddith,
Mubarak bin Muhammad, Al-
- *Jāmi'ul-'Usool li Ahādīth Ar-Rasool* (ed.
Al-Arnout).

Tahāwi, At-
- *Aqīdah At-Tahāwiyyah* (ed. Al-Amout).

Tirmithi, Abī 'Isā Muhammad bin 'Isā bin
Sawrah, At-, (d. 279 н.)
- *Al-Jāmi' As-Sahih*, 5 vols. Beirut: Dār
Al-Fikr, 1983.
- *Sunan At-Tirmithi*.